TOUCH TYPING
SELF-TAUGHT

Nicki Montaperto

BARNES & NOBLE BOOKS
A DIVISION OF HARPER & ROW, PUBLISHERS
New York, Cambridge, Philadelphia, San Francisco
London, Mexico City, São Paulo, Sydney

Illustrations on pp. 8, 16, 34, 35, 37, 39, 42, 45, 48, 51, 54, 57, 60, 63, 66, 69, 72, 77, 83, 85, 87, 89, 91, 93 are here reproduced courtesy of Smith-Corona Group of SCM Corporation.

FIRST EDITION

Library of Congress Cataloging in Publication Data

Montaperto, Nicki.
    Touch typing self-taught.

    (Everyday handbook ; EH/567)
    1. Typewriting. I. Title.
Z49.M78 1983   652.3   82-48253
ISBN 0-06-463567-8 (pbk.)

---

84 85 86 87 10 9 8 7 6 5 4 3 2

CONTENTS

Introduction

The main purpose of this book is to teach you how to type. If you do a new lesson each day--giving it at least one full hour--you will be touch typing in less than a month. If that pace is too fast for you, relax. You're not in a race. You are teaching yourself a valuable skill which is becoming more and more important in the everyday lives of many, many people. You will find uses for your typing skills for the rest of your life, so take whatever time you need to learn them well.

Don't skip any part of any lesson. Wait until you are strong in every part of a lesson before going on to the next.

Moving on too quickly will cause defi-
ciencies that will affect speed and
accuracy later on.

Once you have learned the keyboard,
you will want to begin to put your new
skill to work in various ways according
to your individual needs. For this reason, basic forms for business, school,
and personal use are included in this
book. Use them for practice and reference.

You will also want to know all parts
of your typewriter and the different
features designed to help produce neat
typing. All these features and their
uses are explained in full detail with
practice exercises to help you understand
their function.

To round out your skill so that you
will have a solid base for most of your
everyday typing needs, several typing
aids are explained in detail including
correcting materials, different types of
ribbon available and their uses, copy
stands, and other useful items that will
help make typing easier and neater.

The important thing to remember is that typing is a skill that <u>can</u> be self-taught, even at young ages. The more serious you are about it, and the more you practice, the more quickly you will learn. And that is the key word--practice, practice, practice each lesson thoroughly and patiently and you will succeed.

Good luck!

1

Description of Equipment

KINDS OF TYPEWRITERS

As you begin your lessons in typing, you will be using one of the two kinds of typewriter manufactured today--either a manual or electric typewriter.

Manual or non-electric typewriters come in either portable or standard sizes. A manual typewriter has no automatic features. The characters are mounted on thin, metal rods controlled from the keyboard. When a key is pressed, the corresponding rod strikes the ribbon against the platen (roller) to imprint the character on the page. The carriage moves one space to the left each time a key is struck.

Typing on a manual typewriter requires a firm, sharp stroke with the tips of the fingers pushing down from a curved position. A firm stroke does not have to slow you down. Speeds of 100 words per minute and more have been reached on manual typewriters. These machines also have the convenience of complete portability because the only power they need is you.

Electric typewriters run on electricity. Consequently, many features, including the carriage return, are automated, meaning they repeat automatically when a key is held down. These features will be described in various lessons throughout this book.

A light touch is required in typing, using the flat pads of the fingers rather than the tips as with a manual typewriter.

There are now two kinds of electric typewriters made:

1. Standard electric. Like the manual typewriter, the keys on the standard electric typewriter are mounted on

metal rods. The entire carriage moves
to the left during typing.

2. <u>Single Element Electric (or
Selectric).</u> In this newer kind of typewriter, instead of individual rods, the
characters are mounted on a metal ball
which spins on a shaft as each key is
struck to imprint the letters on the page.
On this kind of typewriter, the carriage
does not move--only the ribbon carrier
and typing ball move across the page during typing.

As with the standard electric typewriter, it requires a light touch using
the pads of the fingertips. It also has
many features to compensate for the stationary carriage, especially the indexer
and express backspacer. These features
will be described in future lessons with
full explanations of their uses.

DESCRIPTION OF TYPEWRITER PARTS

Before you begin to type, it is important to know the parts of your typewriter
and the function of each part. After
learning the basic parts described in

this book, consult the instruction manual to learn about extra or special features built into your own typewriter.

Because the features and operations of manual and electric typewriters differ in some ways, they will be illustrated and described separately for clarity.

MANUAL TYPEWRITER PARTS (Figure 1)

Back-Space Key. Located on the left or right side of the second row of keys from the top. When pressed, this key will move the carriage back one space at a time.

Carriage. This refers to the entire upper part of the typewriter consisting of the platen or roller and all related parts. During typing, the carriage moves from right to left.

Carriage Release Levers. Two levers on each end of the carriage. These levers release the carriage and permit free movement from side to side, allowing the carriage to be stopped at any point.

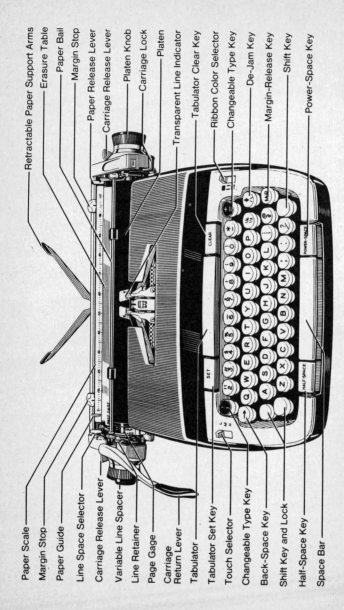

Paper Scale
Margin Stop
Paper Guide
Line Space Selector
Carriage Release Lever
Variable Line Spacer
Line Retainer
Page Gage
Carriage Return Lever
Tabulator
Tabulator Set Key
Touch Selector
Changeable Type Key
Back-Space Key
Shift Key and Lock
Half-Space Key
Space Bar

Retractable Paper Support Arms
Erasure Table
Paper Bail
Margin Stop
Paper Release Lever
Carriage Release Lever
Platen Knob
Carriage Lock
Platen
Transparent Line Indicator
Tabulator Clear Key
Ribbon Color Selector
Changeable Type Key
De-Jam Key
Margin-Release Key
Shift Key
Power-Space Key

Figure 1.   Manual typewriter

Photograph compliments of Smith-Corona Corporation

8

DESCRIPTION OF EQUIPMENT

Carriage Return Lever. A long rod at
the upper left side of the typewriter.
This is used to return the carriage back
to the left hand margin at the end of
each line and to advance the paper up to
the next typing line. It is operated by
pushing the lever with the left hand.

Half-Space Key. This is usually located near the space bar or it is a lever
on top of the typewriter. The half-space
key moves the carriage one half space
backward or forward, depending on the
typewriter. It is used to squeeze in
omitted letters. Not all typewriters
have this feature.

Line Retainer. A small lever either on
the right or left side of the carriage.
This is used to change the line spacing
temporarily. When released, it returns
the roller to the original spacing. This
is used when it is necessary to position
something above or below the normal line
of typing.

Line Space Selector. A small lever
used to set the typewriter for the spacing

needed between lines. These settings
may be for single, double, or triple
spacing. Some typewriters have settings
for one and a half and two and a half
spacing as well.

   Margin-Release Key. A key usually
found on the left side of the top row.
When depressed, it permits the typewriter
to bypass the margins set either on the
right or left side.

   Margin Stops. A key or pair of buttons,
depending on the make of your typewriter,
used to set the width of left and right
margins. To operate, set the typewriter
at the right hand margin chosen and move
the right margin stop to the position.
Repeat for the left margin. The typewriter will now stop and return automatically to these settings.

   Page Gage. A device with markings
built into some typewriters to indicate
the number of inches remaining at the
bottom of the page to prevent typing down
too far. Consult your own instruction
manual to learn how to use this feature

on your particular typewriter.

Paper Bail. A thin metal rod hinged to move against or away from the platen. This is used to hold the paper flat and is aided in this by three small movable rubber rollers strung along the rod.

Paper Release Lever. Usually found on the right side of the typewriter, this lever releases the paper and permits it to be moved freely in any direction or angle. It is also used to straighten the paper after inserting into the typewriter and to position the paper for any unusual angle of typing desired.

Paper Scale. A scale or ruler usually imprinted on the front of the typewriter just above the keys or along the top of the carriage. The marks indicate the number of spaces which are contained across the entire length of the roller,

Platen (also called roller). The hard rubber cylinder which runs the entire width of the carriage to hold the paper in place and provide a backing against which the keys strike in imprinting characters on the page.

Platen Knobs. The knobs on each end
of the roller or platen used to assist
in inserting paper or moving the roller
up and down for vertical spacing on the
page.

Ribbon Color Selector (and Stencil
Adjustment). This adjusts the position
of the ribbon to allow typing on the top
or bottom halves of the ribbon. It is
also used to disengage the ribbon when
typing stencils.

Shift Keys. Found on the right and
left sides of the bottom row, these keys
are used to type capital letters. The
right shift key is used for typing capitals of letters controlled by the left
hand; the left shift key is used for
typing capitals of letters controlled by
the right hand.

Shift Lock. Located just above the
left shift key, this locks the shift so
that only capital letters or upper characters will be typed. It is unlocked by
depressing the left shift key (or either

shift key, depending on the typewriter).

Space Bar. The long bar at the bottom of the keyboard used for spacing between words or moving the carriage to the left. It is operated by the thumb of the right hand.

Tabulator. A key or bar used to indent for paragraphs, columns, or other stops required, such as signatures, dates, or other indentations. Frequently abbreviated as "tab."

Tabulator Clear Key. Used to clear tabulation stops already set, it is operated by tabulating to the stop to be cleared and depressing the key.

Tabulator Set Key. This key is used to set the stops necessary for paragraphs, dates, signatures, columns or other indentations or indexing. It is set by moving the carriage to the stop desired and pressing the tab set key.

Transparent Line Indicator. A small plastic plate marked with lines to assist in lining up with material already typed on the page. It is located at the point

where the ball or keys strike the platen,
directly behind the ribbon. This is
especially useful if the page has been
taken out of the typewriter and must be
reinserted to add or change the typed
text in any way. It also assists in
holding cards in position for typing.

Variable Line Spacer. This mechanism
frees the roller to be turned freely up
or down on the page. It is usually built
into the platen (roller) knob on the left
and is engaged by pushing the knob in
while turning the roller to the desired
position.

FOR ADDITIONAL INFORMATION

This section covers the main parts of
your typewriter which will be used in
learning how to type. For information
about additional features built into
your particular typewriter, consult your
instruction manual. If the instruction
manual is not available, write to the
manufacturer including the model number
of the machine you are using.

ELECTRIC TYPEWRITER PARTS (Figure 2)

Back-Space Key. Located on the left or right side of the top row of keys. When depressed, this key will move the carriage or typing ball back one space at a time.

Repeat Back-Space Key. If the back-space key is automated, it will back-space once if released instantly; if held down, it will continue to backspace until released.

Express Back-Space Key. (not shown) A feature built into some single element or ball typewriters, it moves the typing ball back all the way to the left hand margin or to any point along the way on the same line in one swift, smooth glide rather than in single repeating back spaces. This feature compensates for the stationary carriage by permitting free left and right movement.

Carriage. This refers to the entire upper part of the typewriter consisting of the platen or roller and all related parts. During typing, the carriage moves from left to right on a standard electric

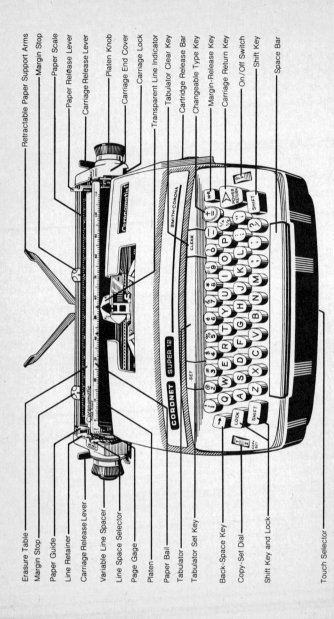

Erasure Table
Margin Stop
Paper Guide
Line Retainer
Carriage Release Lever
Variable Line Spacer
Line Space Selector
Page Gage
Platen
Paper Bail
Tabulator
Tabulator Set Key
Back-Space Key
Copy-Set Dial
Shift Key and Lock
Touch Selector

Retractable Paper Support Arms
Margin Stop
Paper Scale
Paper Release Lever
Carriage Release Lever
Platen Knob
Carriage End Cover
Carriage Lock
Transparent Line Indicator
Tabulator Clear Key
Cartridge Release Bar
Changeable Type Key
Margin-Release Key
Carriage Return Key
On/Off Switch
Shift Key
Space Bar

Figure 2. Electric typewriter

Photograph compliments of
Smith-Corona Corporation

16   DESCRIPTION OF EQUIPMENT

typewriter but remains stationary on a single element electric typewriter.

  Carriage Release Levers. These are two levers on each end of the carriage. The levers release the carriage and permit free movement from side to side, allowing the carriage to be stopped at any point. This feature is not included on a single element electric typewriter. Using the express back spacer and automatic space bar will achieve the same left and right movement of the typing ball.

  Carriage Return Key. A large key found at the right side of the keyboard at the end of the middle rows. It is operated by the small finger of the right hand and is used to advance the paper vertically in the typewriter and also returns the carriage or typing ball to the left hand margin. It moves up in single, double, or triple spacing according to the setting on the Line Space Selector. On some typewriters, this key is automated. Holding it down will cause the paper to continue moving vertically upward until the return key is released.

Indexer Key. (not shown) Built into
some electric typewriters, this key moves
the paper vertically without moving it
horizontally. It is used to form columns
or to line up material typed at the same
setting.

Line Retainer. A small lever either on
the right or left side of the carriage.
This is used to change the line spacing
temporarily. When released, it returns
the roller to the original spacing. This
is used when it is necessary to position
something above or below the normal line
of typing.

Example: It was 12° below zero
when they stopped for the night.

Line Space Selector. A small lever
used to set the typewriter for the spacing
needed between lines. These settings may
be for single, double, or triple spacing.
Some typewriters have settings for one
and a half and two and a half spacing as
well.

Margin Stops. A key or pair of buttons,
depending on the make of your typewriter,
used to set the width of left and right
margins. To operate, set the typewriter
at the right hand margin chosen and move
the right margin stop to that position.
Repeat for the left margin. The typewriter will now stop and return automatically to these settings.

Margin Release Key. Usually found on
the left side of the top row. When depressed, it permits the typewriter to
bypass the margins set either on the left
or right side.

Off and On Switch. Used to turn the
power off and on, this switch is located
either at the right or left of the keyboard, on the side of the typewriter or
under the front side.

Page Gage. A device with markings built
into some typewriters to indicate the
number of inches remaining at the bottom
of the page to prevent typing down too
far. Consult your own instruction manual
to learn how to use this feature on your

particular typewriter.

Paper Bail. A thin metal rod hinged to move against or away from the platen. This is used to hold the paper flat and is aided in this by three small movable rubber rollers strung along the rod.

Paper Guide. A vertical metal strip or bar on the carriage used to guide the left edge of the paper as it is inserted into the typewriter.

Paper Release Lever. Usually found on the right side of the typewriter, this lever releases the paper and permits it to be moved freely in any direction or angle. It is also used to straighten the paper after inserting into the typewriter and to position the paper for any unusual angle of typing desired.

Paper Scale. A scale or ruler usually imprinted on the front of the typewriter just above the keys or along the top of the carriage. The marks indicate the number of spaces which are contained across the entire length of the roller.

<u>Platen (also called roller).</u> The hard
rubber cylinder which runs the entire
width of the carriage to hold the paper
in place and provide a backing against
which the keys strike in imprinting
characters on the page.

<u>Platen Knobs.</u> The knobs on each end
of the roller or platen used to assist
in inserting paper or moving the roller
up and down for vertical spacing on the
page.

<u>Ribbon Color Selector (and Stencil
Adjustment).</u> (not shown) This adjusts
the position of the ribbon to allow typing
on the top or bottom halves of the ribbon.
It is also used to disengage the ribbon
when typing stencils. This lever is
usually located at the left or right side
of the keyboard or is a slide bar under
the ribbon cartridge carrier.

<u>Shift Keys.</u> Found on the bottom row,
these keys are used to type capital
letters. The right shift key is used for
typing capitals of letters controlled by
the left hand; the left shift key is used

for typing capitals of letters controlled by the right hand.

Shift Lock. Located just above the left shift key, this locks the shift so that only capital letters or upper characters will be typed. It is unlocked by depressing one of the shift keys.

Space Bar. The long bar at the bottom of the keyboard used for spacing between words or moving the carriage or typing ball to the left. It is operated by the thumb of the right hand.

Automatic Space Bar. A feature used to move the carriage or typing ball rapidly toward the margin. On most typewriters, it is built directly into the space bar and is engaged by holding the space bar down until reaching the desired place. Some typewriters have a separate Automatic Space Bar. The automatic spacing is stopped by releasing the bar.

Half-Space Key. This is located either near the space bar or on top of the typewriter. The half-space key moves the carriage or typing ball a half space back or forward, depending on the typewriter. It is used to squeeze in omitted letters. Not all typewriters have this feature.

Tabulator. A key or bar used to indent for paragraphs, columns or other stops required, such as signatures, dates, or other indentations.

Tabulator Clear Key. Used to clear tabulation stops already set, it is operated by tabulating to the stop to be cleared and depressing the key.

Tabulator Set Key. This key is used to set the stops necessary for paragraphs, dates, signatures, columns or other indentations or indexing. It is set by moving the carriage to the stop desired and pressing the tab set key.

Transparent Line Indicator. A small plastic plate marked with lines to assist in lining up with material already typed on the page. It is located at the point where the ball or keys strike the platen, directly behind the ribbon. This is especially useful if the page has been taken out of the typewriter and must be

reinserted to add or change the typed
text in any way. It also assists in
holding cards in position for typing.

Variable Line Spacer. This mechanism
frees the roller to be turned freely up
or down on the page. It is usually built
into the platen (roller) knob on the left
and is engaged by pushing the knob in
while turning the roller to the desired
position.

OTHER AUTOMATIC KEYS

To facilitate typing, various keys
have been automated on electric-model
typewriters. Like the repeat back-space
key, index key, space bar, and carriage
return, these keys will repeat automatically when held down and will stop
when released. These automatic keys
include:

Dash. --------Used for crossing out.

Underscore. _____Used for underlining.

Period. ....Used for dotted lines.

X. xxxxxxxxx Used for crossing out.

FOR ADDITIONAL INFORMATION

This section covers the main parts of
your typewriter which will be used in
learning how to type. For information
about additional features built into your
particular typewriter, consult your instruction manual. If the instruction
manual is not available, write to the
manufacturer including the model number
of the machine you are using.

2
Learning How to Type

The purpose of knowing touch typing is to be able to type without looking at the keys. An illustration of the keyboard at the beginning of each new lesson will aid you in locating the position of each new key which is introduced. Look only at the printed keyboard--not down at your fingers.

I strongly recommend that you cover the typewriter keys with small pieces of tape for the first six months of typing. This will strengthen your touch typing skill right from the start and will insure that you don't become dependent on being able to see the keys you need. This was the method I used in learning how to type when I was ten years old. It has since helped people of all ages learn the skill of touch typing.

In the following lessons, all the letters and characters will be systematically introduced, beginning with the home keys and progressing to the keys controlled by each finger. The number keys will be introduced with each lesson as the exercises for each finger are introduced. This will offset the tendency of many self-taught typists to skip the numbers lessons, and avert a permanent weakness in your newly acquired skill.

A progress evaluation form follows each lesson. Use this form to locate and strengthen any weaknesses you may have before you go on to the next lesson.

Please note that some lessons will be divided into separate exercises to accommodate the differences between manual and electric typewriters. These differences occur mostly in the type of operation (manual return vs. electric return, etc.) and in the position of symbols and numbers (hyphen, underscore, quotation marks, apostrophe, etc.)

GETTING STARTED

Setting up your typewriter

Place your typewriter on a table ap-
proximately 27 inches high, the height
of most typing tables or desks. If a
table of this height is not available,
place a telephone book or pillow on your
chair to raise you to the proper height
for typing. Your seat should be 7 or 8
inches below the typewriter desk or table.

If you are unable to rest your feet on
the floor while sitting on a book, place
a small footstool under your feet to keep
you well balanced. Even if you are able
to place your feet squarely on the floor,
resting one foot on a stool will aid in
preventing back fatigue and strain when
typing for long periods of time.

Note: An old table may easily be
converted to a perfect typing table by
cutting 3 inches off the legs. Just be
sure that the table you cut down will
allow you ample leg room after it is

lowered.

On the importance of good posture

After setting your typewriter at the
proper typing height as described, it is
important that you sit properly. Set
yourself directly in front of the typewriter with feet firmly on the floor or
on a stool for proper balance. Sit well
back in your chair and keep your body
erect. Arms should hang relaxed and close
to your sides--not out in a winglike
position. Following these easy steps for
good posture will prevent shoulder and
wrist fatigue, especially when typing for
long periods of time.

Setting up your copy material

Place your copy (material to be typed)
at the side of your typewriter, preferably
the right side. Instead of placing the
material down flat, try to use a copy
stand. This will make it easier to copy
and will position the material at a more
comfortable and correct angle for your
eyes, thus preventing eye strain. Copy

stands may be purchased for as little as
two or three dollars or you may make one
by following the instructions on page 235.

Inserting the paper

Set the paper guide on your typewriter
at 0. Place the left edge of your paper
against this guide before you begin to
insert the paper into the typewriter.
Holding the paper with your left hand,
roll it into the typewriter by turning
the roller knob with your right hand.

Straightening the paper

Bring the paper up into the typewriter
until just the edge shows. Using the top
of the ribbon as a lineup guide, move the
carriage from left to right across the
page to determine if it lines up with the
top of the ribbon at all points. If it
does, you may begin typing.

If not, roll the paper up a few spaces.
Pull the Paper Release Lever toward you.
The paper will now move freely in the
typewriter. Straighten the edge and
gently push the Paper Release Lever back

to its original position. Repeating the
instructions above, check the page again
for straightness. Do this until the page
is straight in the typewriter.

Engaging the paper bail and bail rollers

Roll the paper up a few inches until
you have reached the point where you wish
to begin typing. Raise the paper bail
and position the bail rollers at the
sides and middle of the paper. Press
the paper bail against the paper to hold
it firmly against the roller.

Setting your margins

Decide at which points you wish to begin and end your line of type. Bring the
typewriter to the left margin you have
chosen and set the left margin. Move the
carriage or typing ball to the right hand
margin you have chosen and set the right
hand margin. As you are typing, a little
bell will warn you a few spaces before
approaching the right hand margin and the
end of that line.

Before setting your margins, you should be aware that typewriters are made with two basic type sizes--pica and elite. Pica has 10 spaces to the inch. Elite is a smaller type which has 12 spaces per inch. This is important to know in setting up various kinds of work (tabulations, etc.) when you must know how many spaces you have on a line.

For the lessons in this book, set margins at 10 and 70 for pica and 15 and 80 for elite.

Positioning your hands

Place your fingers on the home keys as illustrated on the next page, using the finger numbers indicated for each key:

Left hand	a s d f	Right hand	j k l ;
Finger number	4 3 2 1	Finger number	1 2 3 4

Thumbs rest lightly on the space bar. The space bar is struck with the right thumb.

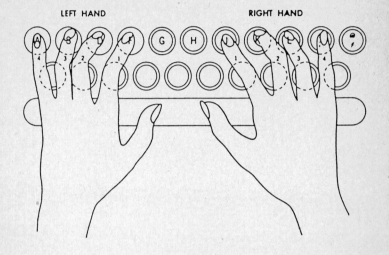

You are now ready for your first lesson.

Lesson 1

HOME KEYS

a   s   d   f   j   k   l   ;

left fingers   right fingers

4   3   2   1   1   2   3   4

<u>Line Selector:</u> Set on 2 for double spacing

<u>Margins:</u> Pica - 10 and 70   Elite - 15 and 80

   Refer to the above picture. With your left
hand, rest your fingers on the keys a s d f
using the fingers indicated. With your right
hand, rest your fingers on keys j k l ; using
the correct finger on each key as indicated.
Thumbs rest lightly on the space bar.

   The eight keys in this lesson are known as

LEARNING HOW TO TYPE

the "home" keys or guide keys. Place your fingers on these home keys anytime you begin to type. As you strike other keys with each finger, you will always return that finger to its proper place on the home keys. Fingers not typing remain in their home key positions.

Begin this lesson by striking the home keys one at a time. Push your finger down firmly and sharply with each stroke. Release as soon as the key strikes the paper.

When striking the keys, many students have found that saying each key aloud with striking has provided additional reinforcement in learning the position. Try this to see if it works for you.

```
 fffffffffjjjjjjjjdddddddddkkkkkkkkksssssssssllllllll
aaaaaaaa;;;;;;;;ssssssssslllllllldddddddddkkkkkkkk
fffffffffjjjjjjjjaaaaaaaa;;;;;;;;llllllllssssssss
dddddddddkkkkkkkkjjjjjjjjffffffffffdddddddddkkkkkkkk
```

Repeat the above lines until you have the feel of striking the keys. Try to keep an even rhythm.

RETURNING THE CARRIAGE

Manual Typewriter

As you reach the end of a line, return the
carriage by using your left hand to push the
Carriage Return Lever firmly and quickly back to
the left margin. Continue typing.

Electric Typewriter

On an electric typewriter with an automatic
carriage return, move the fourth finger on your
right hand and press the Carriage Return Key
firmly. The carriage or typing ball will return
to the left hand margin. Return the fourth finger quickly back to the semi-colon (;) key and
continue typing.

If your electric typewriter does not have an
automatic Carriage Return Key, use the Carriage
Return Lever in the same way as described for
manual typewriters.

USING THE SPACE BAR

Strike the space bar with a quick, light
touch using only your right thumb.

For practice with the space bar, try the
following groupings, leaving a space between

each group.

```
fffffff jjjjjjj ddddddd kkkkkkk sssssss lllllll
aaaaaaa ;;;;;;; ddddddd kkkkkkk aaaaaaa ;;;;;;;
jjjjjjj lllllll sssssss jjjjjjj fffffff dddddddd
fff jjj ddd kkk sss lll aaa ;;; jjj ddd kkk sss
lll aaa ;;; fff kkk sss jjj fff aaa lll ;;; ddd
jfj kdk lsl ;a; fjf dkd sls a;a aja sjs djd fjf
;f; lfl kfk jfj s;s sls sks sjs lal lsl ldl lfl
djd dkd dld d;d kfk kdk ksk kak fjf fkf flf f;f
jfj jdj jsj jaj fds asd jkl ;lk dsa kl; saf l;j
```

Repeat the above exercise five times or until
you complete with no errors.

REMEMBER TO KEEP YOUR EYES ON THE COPY. DO NOT
LOOK AT YOUR TYPEWRITER KEYS.

Test your skill

Repeat the following lines five times or until
you complete with no errors.

```
fad lad dad sad all fall ask lass falls flask as
lads dads fads as alas fads sal jal flasks sass
a sad lad; a sad lass; all dads ask lads; ask a
lass; jal asks; sal asks dad; a dad asks a lass;
```

Self evaluation

Type the following exercise at least one time.

a dad; a lad; a lass; a lad asks; a lass asks;
jad asks; a lad asks a lad; a lass asks dad; a
flask falls; a lad falls; dad falls; jal asks
dad; a flask; a lass; a lad; a fall; sal asks

After each self evaluation:

1) Proofread and circle all errors.

2) On the chart following each self evaluation, note the number of times each letter was
struck incorrectly. This will tell you which
letters need more practice.

Notice if any letter must be counted as an
error many times. If so, go back and repeat the
exercises for that key until it has been mastered.

3) If you have more than two errors in typing
the self evaluation, it is recommended that you
repeat the exercise and evaluate yourself again.

SELF EVALUATION CHART
Lesson 1

Home key row	a	s	d	f			j	k	l	;			
1st evaluation													
2nd evaluation													
3rd evaluation													

Lesson 2

g   h

left finger #1   right finger #1

<u>Line Selector:</u> Set on 2 for double spacing

<u>Margin:</u> Pica - 10 and 70   Elite - 15 and 80

When striking the new keys g and h, or any other new key introduced, remember to return your fingers to the proper home keys.

Repeat the following exercise five times or until you complete with no errors.

```
ggg hhh ggg hhh g h g h f g f g j h j h fgf jhj
dgf khj jhj fgf dgd khk sgs lhl aga ;h; fgf jhj
jgj fhf kgk dhd lgl shs ;g; aha hfh gjg hdh gkg
```

REMEMBER TO KEEP YOUR EYES ON THE COPY.   DO NOT
LOOK AT YOUR KEYS.

Test your skill

Repeat the following line five times or until you
complete with no errors.

fad hag lag ask had gas lass shad fall shall jag
shag flask sad all gall hall dad glass jags fads
flasks falls hags asks lads sal sass gad flag as

Self evaluation

Type the following exercise at least one time.
Be sure to keep your eyes on the copy at all
times--not on the keys.

a lad shall ask a lad; a lad had a fall; a sad
lad; a hag asks a dad; a dad had a flag; a lass
asks a sad lad; a glass falls; a glass flask; a
hag has gall; jad has a gag; sal has a sad dad;

   1) Proofread and circle all errors. Enter in
the chart for Lesson 2.
   2) Note letters repeatedly struck incorrectly.
   3) If there are more than two errors, repeat
and evaluate yourself again.

SELF EVALUATION CHART

Lesson 2

Home key row	a	s	d	f	g	h	j	k	l	;			
1st evaluation													
2nd evaluation													
3rd evaluation													

Lesson 3

r   v   u   m

left finger #1   right finger #1

Line Selector: Set on 2 for double spacing

Margins: Pica - 10 and 70   Elite - 15 and 80

Repeat the following exercise five times or until
you complete with no errors.

rrr vvv uuu mmm rrr vvv uuu mmm rrr vvv uuu mmm

rrr vvv uuu mmm rrr vvv uuu mmm rrr vvv uuu mmm

rfr rdr rsr rar vfv vdv vsv vav uju uku ulu u;u

mjm mkm mlm m;m rjr rkr rlr r;r ufu udu usu uau

vgv vhv rgr rhr mhm mgm uhu ugu uhu rgr mhm vgv

rgr uhu vgv mhm rfr uju vfv mjm rdr uku vdv mkm

REMEMBER TO KEEP YOUR EYES ON THE COPY. RETURN
FINGERS QUICKLY TO THE HOME KEYS.

Test your skill

Repeat the following lines five times or until
you complete with no errors.

rum sum gum hum vum glum far mar jar hard lard
rural mural vagal dam ram jam ham sam vam mask
musk ark mark murk mall dull hull mull lull full

Self evaluation

Type the following exercise at least one time.
Be sure to keep your eyes on the copy at all
times--not on the keys.

a lad has gum; dad hums; a lass had a mask; a
glum gull; gulls ram a dam; a lad had a jar; a
lass had a mark; val hums; a lard jar; a dull
mark; a hard hull; sal had gum; val had a mask;

    1) Proofread and circle all errors. Enter
in the chart for Lesson 3.
    2) Note letters repeatedly struck incorrectly.
    3) If more than two errors, repeat and
evaluate yourself again.

SELF EVALUATION CHART

Lesson 3

2nd row from top				r			u						
1st evaluation													
2nd evaluation													
3rd evaluation													
Home key row	a	s	d	f	g	h	j	k	l	;			
1st evaluation													
2nd evaluation													
3rd evaluation													
Bottom row				v			m						
1st evaluation													
2nd evaluation													
3rd evaluation													

LEARNING HOW TO TYPE

Lesson 4

```
     t    b                              y    n
left finger #1                    right finger #1
```

<u>Line Selector:</u> Set on 2 for double spacing

<u>Margins:</u> Pica - 10 and 70   Elite - 15 and 80

Repeat the following exercise five times or until
completed with no errors.

```
ttt yyy bbb nnn ttt bbb yyy nnn ttt bbb yyy nnn
ttt bbb yyy nnn ttt bbb yyy nnn ttt bbb yyy nnn
yjy yky yly y;y njn nkn nln n;n yjy yky yly y;y
yfy ydy ysy yay bjb bkb blb b;b nfn ndn nsn nan
```

Test your skill

Repeat the following lines five times or until you complete with no errors.

tug a raft; try a bun; a rusty bar sank; many
lads sang; a lass must laugh; a lad and lass
sang hard and funny; dad had a bat and ball; fry
a shad; a lass hangs a flag; a sunny day; mad lad;

KEEP YOUR EYES ON THE COPY. DO NOT LOOK AT THE
KEYS.

Self evaluation

Type the following exercise at least one time.

a sunny day; a lad hunts; a gun bangs; just a
fun gun; a lass bunts a ball; a runt runs afar;
a lass at a mall; just a small mall; try hard;
a vast land; dad had a ham; jan had a small van;

  1) Proofread and circle all errors. Mark
chart for Lesson 4.
  2) Note letters repeatedly struck incorrectly.
  3) If more than two errors, repeat practice
exercise and evaluate yourself again.

SELF EVALUATION CHART

Lesson 4

2nd row from top				r	t	y	u					
1st evaluation												
2nd evaluation												
3rd evaluation												

Home key row	a	s	d	f	g	h	j	k	l	;		
1st evaluation												
2nd evaluation												
3rd evaluation												

Bottom row				v	b	n	m					
1st evaluation												
2nd evaluation												
3rd evaluation												

Lesson 5

4   5   6   7

left finger #1   right finger #1

<u>Line Selector:</u> Set on 2 for double spacing

<u>Margins:</u> Pica - 10 and 70   Elite - 15 and 80

Repeat the following lines five times or until
completed with no errors. Remember to return
fingers to home keys after striking.

444 666 555 777 444 777 555 666 777 444 666 555
777 444 777 555 444 777 555 666 444 666 777 555
666 444 777 555 666 555 777 444 666 777 555 444
4f4 4d4 4s4 4a4 6j6 6k6 616 6;6 5f5 5d5 5s5 5a5
7j7 7k7 717 7;7 4j4 5j5 6f6 7f7 555 666 444 777

Test your skill

Repeat the following lines five times or until
you complete with no errors.

a lass bats 5 balls; a dad has 4 rafts; a lad
has 7 jars; 5 days; 56 hams; 74 lads; 75 maps;
4 vans; 7 grass mats; 64 funny guns; 6 tugs;
7 sunny days; 4 saggy dads; 6 musty barns; 4 rats;

Self evaluation

Type the following lines at least one time.

a sunny day; a glum lass; a sad lad; a lad runs
fast; a lass had jam; a dad had 45 hats and 67
lads; 45 glad lads had hats; mad lads; 4 balls;
6 bats; 7 runs; hats are funny; days are sunny;
hang a ratty hat; a numb hand; a hard try; a bad
jam; 565 bands; 47 flags; 7 lads and 7 lasses;

KEEP YOUR EYES ON THE COPY AT ALL TIMES. DO NOT
LOOK AT THE KEYS.

   1) Proofread and circle all errors. Enter
on chart for Lesson 5.

   2) Note letters repeatedly struck incorrectly
and practice again.

   3) If more than two errors, repeat practice

exercise and evaluate yourself again.

SELF EVALUATION CHART
Lesson 5

Top row				4	5	6	7					
1st evaluation												
2nd evaluation												
3rd evaluation												

2nd row from top				r	t	y	u					
1st evaluation												
2nd evaluation												
3rd evaluation												

Home key row	a	s	d	f	g	h	j	k	l	;			
1st evaluation													
2nd evaluation													
3rd evaluation													

Bottom row				v	b	n	m					
1st evaluation												
2nd evaluation												
3rd evaluation												

　　　　　　　　　　LEARNING HOW TO TYPE

Lesson 6

e   c   i   ,

left finger #2   right finger #2

<u>Line Selector:</u> Set on 2 for double spacing

<u>Margins:</u> Pica - 10 and 70   Elite - 15 and 80

Repeat five times or until you complete with no
errors.

eee iii ccc ,,, eee iii ,,, ccc eee iii ccc ,,,
eee ccc iii ,,, efe ede ese eae iji iki ili i;i
,j, ,k, ,l, ,;, eje eke ele e;e ifi idi isi iai
,f, ,d, ,s, ,a, efe ede ese eae iji iki ili i;i
eie e,e iei ici cic c,c ,e, ,c, i,i ece cic ,e,

Test your skill

Repeat 5 times. REMEMBER TO KEEP YOUR EYES ON
THE COPY. RETURN FINGERS QUICKLY TO HOME KEYS.

men ten hen den, sin tin gin fin, mat bat sat
cat hat rat, man can fan tan ban, must rust bust
lust gust dust, kite mite rite bite cite site
invite trite, dike hike bike mike, mine tine
line fine brine, dime time grime lime, like dike
hike, brim trim, brink sink link mink, brine mine

Self evaluation

Type at least one time.

4 men sit still; the 5th girl hits hard; 6 lads
catch flies; 7 kites fly high; try a last time;
strike the line; let it sit; sunny days are
bright, rainy days are dark, misty days are dim;

1) Proofread and circle all errors. Enter
on chart for Lesson 6.

2) Note letters repeatedly struck incorrectly
and practice again.

3) If more than two errors, repeat practice
exercise and evaluate yourself again.

SELF EVALUATION CHART

Lesson 6

Top row				4	5	6	7						
1st evaluation													
2nd evaluation													
3rd evaluation													
2nd row from top			e	r	t	y	u	i					
1st evaluation													
2nd evaluation													
3rd evaluation													
Home key row	a	s	d	f	g	h	j	k	l	;			
1st evaluation													
2nd evaluation													
3rd evaluation													
Bottom row			c	v	b	n	m	,					
1st evaluation													
2nd evaluation													
3rd evaluation													

Lesson 7

3

left finger #2

8

right finger #2

Line Selector: Set on 2 for double spacing

Margins: Pica - 10 and 70   Elite - 15 and 80

Repeat five times or until you complete with no errors.

333 888 333 888 333 888 333 888 333 888 333 888
f3f d3d s3s a3a j8j k8k 18l ;8; 8f8 8d8 8s8 8a8
3j3 3k3 313 3;3 343 353 363 373 383 878 868 858
848 838 888 333 878 343 868 353 838 383 888 333

Test your skill

Repeat five times or until you complete with no errors.

best test rest lest jest, turn burn churn, mean
bean lean, bunny funny, star mar bar tar jar,
card lard bard, hay say may day, main rain gain
train grain, veer beer seer jeer, ear hear, here
363, 474, 838, 565, 575, 383, 454, 484, 585, 686

Self evaluation

Type at least one time. REMEMBER TO KEEP YOUR
EYES ON THE COPY.

5 men ate fish; 4 lines held the fish; a raft
ran the river; the best 3 fish ran far; the men
tried hard, but failed; they ate the fish they
caught; 8 girls had bats and balls; they came
early; they tried hard for the first 6 innings;
the game tied at 7 runs in the last inning; they
hit a ball hard and made the tie breaking run;

   1) Proofread and circle all errors. Mark
the chart for Lesson 7.
   2) Note letters repeatedly struck incorrectly
and practice those lessons again.
   3) If more than two errors, repeat practice

exercise and evaluate yourself again.

SELF EVALUATION CHART

Lesson 7

Top row			3	4	5	6	7	8					
1st evaluation													
2nd evaluation													
3rd evaluation													
2nd row from top			e	r	t	y	u	i					
1st evaluation													
2nd evaluation													
3rd evaluation													
Home key row	a	s	d	f	g	h	j	k	l	;			
1st evaluation													
2nd evaluation													
3rd evaluation													
Bottom row			c	v	b	n	m	,					
1st evaluation													
2nd evaluation													
3rd evaluation													

Lesson 8

w   x   o   .

left finger #3   right finger #3

<u>Line Selector:</u> Set on 2 for double spacing

<u>Margins:</u> Pica - 10 and 70   Elite - 15 and 80

Repeat five times or until you complete with no errors.

www ooo xxx ... www ooo xxx ... www ooo xxx ...
www ooo xxx ... www ooo xxx ... www ooo xxx ...
wfw wdw wsw waw ojo oko olo o;o xfx xdx xsx xax
.j. .k. .l. .;. wgw oho xgx .h. wgw xgx oho .h.

Test your skill

Repeat five times or until you complete with no errors.

bone hone gone long vote rote wrote tote foam
loam some come will bill hill trill mill mix
nix elixir went bent rent lent extent sent cent
exit extra exist exact extract kick lick ax ox
st., ave., rd., dr., mr., mrs., ms., jr., sr.,
etc., i.e., e.g., bldg., blvd., lb., in., ft.,

Self evaluation

Type at least one time. REMEMBER TO KEEP YOUR
EYES ON THE COPY.

the boys went to a farm. they found some cows
and milked them. the cows were extra tired.
when the boys milked them, they balked. the
girls went to a movie. they had seen the film
before. they tried to get their money back, but
the manager did not agree. the girls saw the
film again. some people waste time and some
waste money. some people waste time and money
both, but are having fun so they make extra money
and spend more time.

    1) Proofread and circle all errors.

58   LEARNING HOW TO TYPE

2) Note letters repeatedly struck incorrectly and practice again.

3) If more than two errors, repeat practice exercise and evaluate yourself again.

SELF EVALUATION CHART

Lesson 8

Top row		3	4	5	6	7	8					
1st evaluation												
2nd evaluation												
3rd evaluation												

2nd row from top		w	e	r	t	y	u	i	o			
1st evaluation												
2nd evaluation												
3rd evaluation												

Home key row	a	s	d	f	g	h	j	k	l	;		
1st evaluation												
2nd evaluation												
3rd evaluation												

Bottom row		x	c	v	b	n	m	,	.			
1st evaluation												
2nd evaluation												
3rd evaluation												

Lesson 9

2   9

left finger #3   right finger #3

Line Selector: Set on 2 for double spacing

Margins: Pica - 10 and 70   Elite - 15 and 80

Repeat five times or until you complete with no
errors.

222 999 222 999 222 999 222 999 292 929 299 922

2f2 2d2 2s2 2a2 9j9 9k9 919 9;9 9f9 9d9 9s9 9a9

2j2 2k2 2l2 2;2 2g2 9h9 2h2 9g9 222 999 292 929

232 242 252 262 272 282 989 979 969 959 949 939

929 939 949 959 292 282 272 262 293 928 243 978

Test your skill

Repeat five times or until you complete with no errors.

two 2 three 3 four 4 five 5 six 6 seven 7 eight 8 nine 9 rate mate hate late date dream cream beam team ream seam try cry fry dry high sigh light sight might right fight height weight freight

KEEP YOUR EYES ON THE COPY AT ALL TIMES. DO NOT LOOK AT THE KEYS.

Self evaluation

Type at least one time.

we want to call home. the number is 245 3892. the address is 789 5th avenue. the cost for each minute is 3 dollars. we will write a letter instead. when we write a letter, we say less and spend less too. the best way to learn numbers is to do them over and over again. 2, 3, 4, 5, 6, 7, 8, 9. when they are learned well, they are easy forever.

   1) Proofread and circle all errors. Enter on chart for Lesson 9.
   2) Note letters repeatedly struck incorrectly and practice again.

3) If more than two errors, repeat practice exercise and evaluate yourself again.

SELF EVALUATION CHART

Lesson 9

Top row		2	3	4	5	6	7	8	9			
1st evaluation												
2nd evaluation												
3rd evaluation												
2nd row from top		w	e	r	t	y	u	i	o			
1st evaluation												
2nd evaluation												
3rd evaluation												
Home key row	a	s	d	f	g	h	j	k	l	;		
1st evaluation												
2nd evaluation												
3rd evaluation												
Bottom row		x	c	v	b	n	m	,	.			
1st evaluation												
2nd evaluation												
3rd evaluation												

Lesson 10

q   z   p   /

left finger #4   right finger #4

<u>Line Selector:</u> Set on 2 for double spacing

<u>Margins:</u> Pica - 10 and 70   Elite - 15 and 80

Repeat five times or until you complete with no
errors.

qqq ppp zzz /// qqq ppp zzz /// qqq ppp zzz ///
qqq ppp zzz /// qqq ppp zzz /// qqq ppp zzz ///
qfq qdq qsq qaq pjp pkp plp p;p zfz zdz zsz zaz
/j/ /k/ /l/ /;/ qgq qhq php pgp zgz zhz /h/ /g/

LEARNING HOW TO TYPE   63

Test your skill

Repeat five times or until you complete with no errors.

quit quite query merry/terry zero zest zebra
zany zoo ooze doze dozen paste/waste/baste
kept/inept/swept/slept helped/yelped gulped
slurped mapped super supper trip/rip/drip/flip/
hip/whip/zip zone/bone/hone/atone narrow/arrow

REMEMBER TO RETURN FINGERS QUICKLY TO HOME KEYS.

Self evaluation

Type at least one time. LOOK ONLY AT THE COPY.
DO NOT LOOK AT THE KEYS.

the squire and the lady went for a ride. his
horse was quite wild, but the squire wanted to
show off. he put the spurs to his horse hard.
the horse stopped short. the unhappy squire
flew up, over and down. the lady was not
impressed, but she loved the squire anyway. the
squire was dazed but happy. 3/4 of the class
passed the test and 1/4 failed. 1/2 tried again.

   1) Proofread and circle all errors. Enter
on chart for Lesson 10.

2) Note letters repeatedly struck incorrectly and practice again.

3) If more than two errors, repeat practice exercise and evaluate yourself again.

SELF EVALUATION CHART

Lesson 10

Top row		2	3	4	5	6	7	8	9			
1st evaluation												
2nd evaluation												
3rd evaluation												

2nd row from top	q	w	e	r	t	y	u	i	o	p			
1st evaluation													
2nd evaluation													
3rd evaluation													

Home key row	a	s	d	f	g	h	j	k	l	;			
1st evaluation													
2nd evaluation													
3rd evaluation													

Bottom row	z	x	c	v	b	n	m	,	.	/			
1st evaluation													
2nd evaluation													
3rd evaluation													

1   0

left finger #4   right finger #4

(if your typewriter does not
have #1 in the top row, use
small L (1) for number one
instead. Strike with third
finger as usual.)

<u>Line Selector:</u> Set on 2 for double spacing

<u>Margins:</u> Pica - 10 and 70   Elite - 15 and 80

Repeat five times or until you complete with no
errors.

111 000 111 000 111 000 111 000 111 000 111 000

1f1 1d1 1s1 1a1 0j0 0k0 0l0 0;0 1g1 0h0 101 010

701 510 105 410 102 301 890 901 106 601 710 101

<u>Note:</u> It is important that you do all the exer-
cises in this lesson with your eyes on the copy
at all times. Do not be tempted to look at your
keys. These exercises should be repeated over
and over again until you know the exact position
of each of the number keys by touch alone.

<u>Test your skill</u>

Repeat five times or until you complete with no
errors.

10 days 34 months 17 years 7/10/82 12/14/80
749 5th street 25 days 20 months 14 weeks 78 days
90 pounds 72 hours 1 inch 54 weeks 12 months
5 years 90 hours 30 days 15 percent 2 days

<u>Self evaluation</u>

Type at least one time. DO NOT LOOK AT THE KEYS.

the only way to learn numbers is to practice
them. when you do them, you will know exactly
where each one is without looking at the keys.
the words and phrases will come easily too when
you know the position of each key on the keyboard
by touch alone. then you will have learned touch
typing.

1 week, 6 months, 24 hours, 5 years, 6 decades, 70 people, 89 percent, 22 minutes, 14 weeks, dates of 1/4/73, 12/27/82.

1) Proofread and circle all errors.

2) Note letters and numbers repeatedly struck incorrectly and practice again.

3) If there are more than two errors, repeat and evaluate yourself again.

SELF EVALUATION CHART
Lesson 11

Top row	1	2	3	4	5	6	7	8	9	0			
1st evaluation													
2nd evaluation													
3rd evaluation													

2nd row from top	q	w	e	r	t	y	u	i	o	p			
1st evaluation													
2nd evaluation													
3rd evaluation													

Home key row	a	s	d	f	g	h	j	k	l	;			
1st evaluation													
2nd evaluation													
3rd evaluation													

Bottom row	z	x	c	v	b	n	m	,	.	/			
1st evaluation													
2nd evaluation													
3rd evaluation													

Lesson 12

FOR MANUAL TYPEWRITERS

-      =   ½   ¢

right finger #4

<u>Line Selector:</u> Set on 2 for double spacing

<u>Margins:</u> Pica - 10 and 70   Elite - 15 and 80

Repeat five times or until you complete with no errors.

--- === $\frac{1}{2}\frac{1}{2}\frac{1}{2}$ ¢¢¢ --- === $\frac{1}{2}\frac{1}{2}\frac{1}{2}$ ¢¢¢ --- === $\frac{1}{2}\frac{1}{2}\frac{1}{2}$ ¢¢¢

-j- =j= $\frac{1}{2}$j$\frac{1}{2}$ ¢j¢ -k- =k= $\frac{1}{2}$k$\frac{1}{2}$ ¢k¢ -l- =l= $\frac{1}{2}$l$\frac{1}{2}$ ¢l¢

-f- =f= $\frac{1}{2}$f$\frac{1}{2}$ ¢f¢ -d- =d= $\frac{1}{2}$d$\frac{1}{2}$ ¢d¢ -s- =s= $\frac{1}{2}$s$\frac{1}{2}$ ¢s¢

--- ¢¢¢ === $\frac{1}{2}\frac{1}{2}\frac{1}{2}$ ¢¢¢ === $\frac{1}{2}\frac{1}{2}\frac{1}{2}$ --- === ¢¢¢ $\frac{1}{2}\frac{1}{2}\frac{1}{2}$ ---

Test your skill

Repeat five times or until you complete with no errors.

5¢; 140-20 42nd street; $\frac{1}{2}$ cup milk; 4-5 cups
sugar, 10¢ candy; 12¢, 140-3257; $\frac{1}{2}$ lb. butter;
the 5th day of the month; 6/7/82 = 6-7-82 =
june 7, 1982; $\frac{1}{2}$ dollar; 10 pennies = 1 dime;
5¢ = 1/20th of a dollar; 25¢ = 1/4th of a dollar;

Self evaluation

Type at least one time. KEEP EYES ONLY ON THE
COPY. DO NOT LOOK AT THE KEYS.

the children were baking a cake. they used 2 lbs.
of flour, $3\frac{1}{2}$ cups of milk, 2-2/3 cups of sugar,
4 tbs. of butter. they all mixed the cake and
baked it at 350 degrees. they had a feast and
it only cost 25¢ each.

1) Proofread and circle all errors. Enter on
chart for Lesson 12 (FOR MANUAL TYPEWRITERS).

2) Note letters repeatedly struck incorrectly
and practice again.

3) If more than two errors, repeat practice
exercise and evaluate yourself again.

SELF EVALUATION CHART

Lesson 12

(Manual Typewriters)

Top row	1	2	3	4	5	6	7	8	9	0	–	=	
1st evaluation													
2nd evaluation													
3rd evaluation													

2nd row from top	q	w	e	r	t	y	u	i	o	p	½		
1st evaluation													
2nd evaluation													
3rd evaluation													

Home key row	a	s	d	f	g	h	j	k	l	;	¢		
1st evaluation													
2nd evaluation													
3rd evaluation													

Bottom row	z	x	c	v	b	n	m	,	.	/			
1st evaluation													
2nd evaluation													
3rd evaluation													

Lesson 12

FOR ELECTRIC TYPEWRITERS

$-$ $=$ $\frac{1}{2}$ '

right finger #4

Line Selector: Set on 2 for double spacing

Margins: Pica - 10 and 70   Elite - 15 and 80

Repeat five times or until you complete with no errors.

```
--- === ½½½ ''' --- === ½½½ ''' --- === ½½½ '''
-j- =j= ½j½ 'j' -k- =k= ½k½ 'k' -l- =l= ½l½ 'l'
-f- =f= ½f½ 'f' -d- =d= ½d½ 'd' -s- =s= ½s½ 's'
--- ½½½ ''' === --- ''' ½½½ === ''' ½½½ --- ===
```

Test your skill

Repeat five times or until you complete with no errors.

mother's dad's mom's baby's child's 1/2 = ½
1½ 2½ 3½ 4½ 5½ 6½ 7½ 8½ 9½ 10½ 2-3/4 3-3/4 5-3/4
3 x 4 = 12 4 x 4 = 16 4 5's = 20 1/3 = one-third
half-pint one-half one-fifth 7/8/83 = 7-8-83

Self evaluation

Type at least one time. KEEP YOUR EYES ON THE
COPY. RETURN FINGERS QUICKLY TO HOME KEYS.

the children were baking a cake. they used 2 lbs.
of flour, 3 cups of milk, 2-2/3 cups of sugar,
4 tbs. of butter. they all mixed the cake and
baked it at 350 degrees. they had a feast and
spent less of their parents' money.

1) Proofread and circle all errors. Enter on
chart for Lesson 12 (FOR ELECTRIC TYPEWRITERS).

2) Note keys repeatedly struck incorrectly
and practice again.

3) If more than two errors, repeat practice
exercise and evaluate yourself again.

SELF EVALUATION CHART

Lesson 12

(Electric Typewriters)

Top row	1	2	3	4	5	6	7	8	9	0	-	=	
1st evaluation													
2nd evaluation													
3rd evaluation													

2nd row from top	q	w	e	r	t	y	u	i	o	p	½		
1st evaluation													
2nd evaluation													
3rd evaluation													

Home key row	a	s	d	f	g	h	j	k	l	;	'		
1st evaluation													
2nd evaluation													
3rd evaluation													

Bottom row	z	x	c	v	b	n	m	,	.	/			
1st evaluation													
2nd evaluation													
3rd evaluation													

LEARNING HOW TO TYPE

KEYBOARD PRACTICE

Copy the following paragraph three times for full keyboard and continuous typing practice. If you wish to test your speed, the word count is included at the end of each line. This word count is based on an average of six letters per word--not an actual count of each individual word. After you have typed the entire paragraph, divide the number of minutes into the number of words you have typed to determine the number of words typed per minute. A self evaluation form is included at the end of the exercise to help you measure your progress.

Line Selector: Set on 2 for double spacing

Margins: Pica - 10 and 70   Elite - 15 and 80

you have now been introduced to all the letters and numbers	10
on the keyboard. be sure to keep your eyes on the copy at	20
all times. this will increase your touch typing skill. you	30
should also try to maintain an even typing tempo, striking	40
each key sharply and firmly and releasing quickly. do not	50
worry about speed. it will come with time and patience.	60

Self evaluation

	Words per minute	Number of errors
1st test	_____	_____
2nd test	_____	_____
3rd test	_____	_____

Check your work carefully just as you did in
Lessons 1-12. Notice if any letters are
repeatedly struck incorrectly. Go back to the
lessons covering those letters and practice the
exercises again until you overcome any weakness.
This steady checking and rechecking will make
you a skillful and accurate typist right from
the start.

Lesson 13

Shift Lock Key
left finger #4

Shift Keys
left and right finger #4

The shift key is used to type capital letters or the symbols on the upper half of double marked keys.

To type a capital letter or any of the upper characters, hold the shift key on the opposite side of the keyboard down with the fourth finger, strike the letter to be capitalized and release the shift. Return both hands to home keys as usual.

Note: For capital "A," hold the shift key down with the fourth finger of your right hand as you strike the "a" with your left fourth finger.

LEARNING HOW TO TYPE   77

Repeat five times. Release the shift key quickly
and continue your typing rhythm.

Fay Dad Jay Kay Mom Tom Bob Harriet Nancy Skip
Sally Harry January February March April May
June July August September October November
December Monday Tuesday Wednesday Thursday Friday

Test your skill

Repeat five times or until you complete with no
errors.

The Waverly Company 14 Fifth Avenue Las Vegas,   xx
Nevada   Mary Thomas   George Bernard Shaw
Tennessee Williams   Mary Tyler Moore   Gone With
the Wind by Margaret Mitchell was made into a
3-hour movie. The stars were Vivien Leigh,
Clark Gable and Olivia de Havilland. It was
produced by MGM.

   The shift lock key is used to type solid
capital letters. To lock the shift, press the
shift lock. To release, after typing, press one
of the shift keys.

Test your skill

Repeat the following exercise five times.

The students were required to do a book report.
The instruction sheet noted: AN OUTLINE MUST BE
SUBMITTED AND APPROVED BEFORE THE FINAL REPORT
IS WRITTEN. They all obeyed the instructions.
The teacher was pleased and raised all the
grades. There were five As, 6 Bs and only 1 C.   xx

Speed practice (using capitals)

As you perfect your skill, you will find many everyday uses   10

for typing. School work always looks better when it is   20

typed. Teachers are pleased by neater work. Notes are   30

easier to study when they are typed. This will help improve   40

your grades too. Long letters are fun to write but take too   50

long by hand. Sometimes you might want to type an extra   60

long letter to a friend. Business letters always look better   70

when they are typed and people pay more attention to a typed   80

letter. Later on, you will learn more and more uses for   90

typing. Samples of different forms will show you the many   100

ways you can use this skill in your work, study and play.   110

Self evaluation

One-minute test

	Words per minute	Number of errors
1st evaluation		
2nd evaluation		
3rd evaluation		

Three-minute test

1st evaluation		
2nd evaluation		
3rd evaluation		

LEARNING HOW TO TYPE

Speed practice

Line Selector: Set on 2 for double spacing

Margins: Pica - 10 and 70   Elite - 15 and 80

PUNCTUATION IN TYPING

When typing anything in sentences, the proper spacing after	10
a period is two spaces. Two spaces are also left after a	20
colon, question mark, quotation mark closing a quote and	30
after parentheses ending a sentence. One space is left	40
after a comma or semi-colon. As you do more and more typing,	50
you will begin to leave proper spaces in each case without	60
thinking about it. Using the shift keys and the tab keys	70
will also be done automatically. You will also begin to	80
adapt to the way things should look in type. For example,	90
when setting something off with a colon, you will know it	100
should look this way: Two spaces after a colon and a	110
capital letter to begin the sentence following the colon,	120
exactly the way you have just copied it from this exercise.	130

	Words per minute	Number of errors
One-minute test		
1st evaluation	_____	_____
2nd evaluation	_____	_____
3rd evaluation	_____	_____
Three-minute test		
1st evaluation	_____	_____
2nd evaluation	_____	_____
3rd evaluation	_____	_____

Speed practice

<u>Line Selector:</u> Set on 2 for double spacing

<u>Margins:</u> Pica - 10 and 70   Elite - 15 and 80

PRACTICING SYMBOLS

Take your time with the next three lessons and learn them   10

well. These keys will not get as much practice in regular   20

typing as all the letter keys will. For this reason, you   30

must strengthen your skill with all numbers and symbols   40

during the learning process. Learn them well and they will   50

be yours forever.

	<u>Words per minute</u>	<u>Number of errors</u>
<u>One-minute test</u>		
1st evaluation	_____	_____
2nd evaluation	_____	_____
3rd evaluation	_____	_____
<u>Three-minute test</u>		
1st evaluation	_____	_____
2nd evaluation	_____	_____
3rd evaluation	_____	_____

LEARNING HOW TO TYPE

Lesson 14

FOR MANUAL TYPEWRITERS

Symbols - Top Row Left

	"	#	$	%
Left finger #	3	2	1	1

To type all the above symbols you must hold the right shift key down using your right finger #4.

Type the following lines at least five times.

""" ### $$$ %%% """ ### $$$ %%% """ ### $$$ %%%
""" ### $$$ %%% """ ### $$$ %%% """ ### $$$ %%%
f%f f$f f#f f"f d%d d$d d#d d"d s%s s$s s#s s"s

Press the shift lock down for the next two lines.

%%% $$$ ### """ ### %%% ### """ $$$ ### %%% ###
""" ### %%% $$$ """ ### %%% $$$ """ $$$ %%% ###

LEARNING HOW TO TYPE   83

KEEP YOUR EYES ON THE COPY AT ALL TIMES. DO NOT
LOOK AT THE KEYS. TO LOCATE THE SYMBOLS, USE
THE KEYBOARD ILLUSTRATION.

Repeat the above exercise five times or until
you complete with no errors. Extra practice now
will prevent errors later.

1) Proofread and circle all errors. Enter on
the chart below.

2) Note symbols repeatedly struck incorrectly
and practice again.

3) If more than two errors, repeat practice
exercise and evaluate yourself again.

SELF EVALUATION CHART
Lesson 14
(Manual Typewriters)

Top row	" 2	# 3	$ 4	% 5							
1st evaluation											
2nd evaluation											
3rd evaluation											

LEARNING HOW TO TYPE

Lesson 15

FOR MANUAL TYPEWRITERS

Symbols - Top Row Right

	_	&	'	(	)	*	+
right finger #	1	1	2	3	4	4	4

To type all the above symbols, you must hold the left shift key down using your left finger #4.

Type the following lines at least five times.

___ &&& ''' ((( ))) *** +++ ___ &&& ''' ((( )))
*** +++ ___ &&& ''' ((( ))) *** +++ ___ &&& '''
j_j j&j j'j j(j j)j j*j j+j k_k k&k k'k k(k k)k

Press the shift lock down for the next two lines.

___ &&& ''' ((( ))) *** +++ ((( ))) ''' &&& ___
+++ *** ((( ))) ___ ''' *** +++ &&& ___ ''' ***

LEARNING HOW TO TYPE   85

Repeat the practice exercises five times or until
you complete with no errors.

USE THE KEYBOARD ILLUSTRATION TO LOCATE THE
SYMBOLS. DO NOT LOOK AT YOUR TYPEWRITER KEYBOARD.

1) Proofread and circle all errors. Enter on
the chart below.
2) Note symbols repeatedly struck incorrectly
and practice again.
3) If more than two errors, repeat practice
exercise and evaluate yourself again.

SELF EVALUATION CHART
Lesson 15
(Manual Typewriters)

Top row	" 2	# 3	$ 4	% 5	– 6	& 7	' 8	(9	) 0	* –	+ =	
1st evaluation												
2nd evaluation												
3rd evaluation												

LEARNING HOW TO TYPE

Lesson 16

FOR MANUAL TYPEWRITERS

Symbols - Right End Rows

¼   @   ?

right finger #4

To type all the above symbols, you must hold the
left shift key down using your left finger #4.

Type the following at least five times.

¼¼¼ @@@ ??? ¼¼¼ @@@ ??? ¼¼¼ @@@ ??? ¼¼¼ @@@ ???
¼¼¼ @@@ ??? ¼¼¼ @@@ ??? ¼¼¼ @@@ ??? ¼¼¼ @@@ ???
j¼j j@j j?j k¼k k@k k?k l¼l l@l l?l ;¼; ;@; ;?;

Press the shift lock down for the next two lines.

@@@ ??? ¼¼¼ ??? @@@ ??? ¼¼¼ @@@ ??? ¼¼¼ @@@ ???
¼¼¼ ??? @@@ ??? ¼¼¼ @@@ ¼¼¼ ??? @@@ ??? @@@ ¼¼¼

USE THE KEYBOARD ILLUSTRATION TO LOCATE THE
SYMBOLS. DO NOT LOOK AT YOUR TYPEWRITER KEYBOARD.

Repeat the practice exercises five times or
until you complete with no errors.

1) Proofread and circle all errors. Enter on
the chart below.

2) Note symbols repeatedly struck incorrectly
and practice again.

3) If more than two errors, repeat practice
exercise and evaluate yourself again.

SELF EVALUATION CHART

Lesson 16

(Manual Typewriters)

Top row	"/2	#/3	$/4	%/5	/6	&/7	'/8	(/9	)/0	*/-	+/=		
1st evaluation													
2nd evaluation													
3rd evaluation													
2nd row from top												$\frac{1}{4}$	$\frac{1}{2}$
1st evaluation													
2nd evaluation													
3rd evaluation													
Home key row												@/¢	
1st evaluation													
2nd evaluation													
3rd evaluation													
Bottom row												?	
1st evaluation													
2nd evaluation													
3rd evaluation													

Lesson 14

FOR ELECTRIC TYPEWRITERS
Symbols - Top Row Left

	!	@	#	$	%
Left finger #	4	3	2	1	1

To type all the above symbols, you must hold the right shift key down using your right finger #4.

Type the following lines at least five times.

```
!!! @@@ ### $$$ %%% !!! @@@ ### $$$ %%% !!! @@@
### $$$ %%% !!! @@@ ### $$$ %%% !!! @@@ ### $$$
f%f f$f f#f f@f f!f d%d d$d d#d d@d d!d s%s s$s
```

Press the shift lock down for the next two lines.
```
!!! @@@ ### $$$ !!! ### $$$ @@@ %%% ### !!! ###
$$$ @@@ ### %%% !!! @@@ ### %%% $$$ @@@ ### $$$
```

USE THE KEYBOARD ILLUSTRATION TO LOCATE THE
SYMBOLS. DO NOT LOOK AT YOUR TYPEWRITER KEYBOARD.

Repeat the practice exercises five times or
until you complete with no errors. Extra
practice now will prevent errors later.

1) Proofread and circle all errors. Enter on
the chart below.

2) Note symbols repeatedly struck incorrectly
and practice again.

3) If more than two errors, repeat practice
exercise and evaluate yourself again.

SELF EVALUATION CHART

Lesson 14

(Electric Typewriters)

Top row	!/1	@/2	#/3	$/4	%/5							
1st evaluation												
2nd evaluation												
3rd evaluation												

Lesson 15

FOR ELECTRIC TYPEWRITERS

Symbols - Top Row Right

	¢	&	*	(	)	_	+
right finger #	1	1	2	3	4	4	4

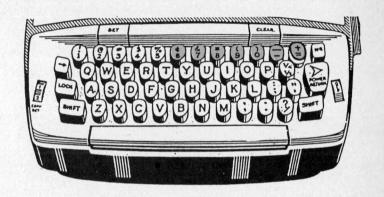

To type the symbols above, you must hold the left
shift key down using your left finger #4.

Type the following lines at least five times.

¢¢¢ &&& *** ((( ))) ___ +++ ¢¢¢ &&& *** ((( )))
___ +++ ¢¢¢ &&& *** ((( ))) ___ +++ ¢¢¢ &&& ***
j¢j j&j j*j j(j j)j j_j j+j k¢k k&k k*k k(k k)k

Press the shift lock key for the next two lines.
¢¢¢ *** &&&))) (((*** ___ +++ *** ¢¢¢ &&& (((
))) ___ *** +++))) ¢¢¢ &&& *** +++ ((( ))) &&&

USE THE KEYBOARD ILLUSTRATION TO LOCATE THE
SYMBOLS. DO NOT LOOK AT YOUR TYPEWRITER KEYS.

Repeat the practice exercises five times or
until you complete with no errors.

1) Proofread and circle all errors. Enter on
the chart below.

2) Note symbols repeatedly struck incorrectly
and practice again.

3) If more than two errors, repeat practice
exercise and evaluate yourself again.

SELF EVALUATION CHART

Lesson 15

(Electric Typewriters)

Top row	! 1	@ 2	# 3	$ 4	% 5	¢ 6	& 7	* 8	(9	) 0	– -	+ =	
1st evaluation													
2nd evaluation													
3rd evaluation													

Lesson 16

FOR ELECTRIC TYPEWRITERS

Symbols - Right End Rows

$\frac{1}{4}$ "   ?

right finger #4

To type all the above symbols, you must hold the left shift key down using your left finger #4.

Type the following lines at least five times.

$\frac{1}{4}\frac{1}{4}\frac{1}{4}$ """ ??? $\frac{1}{4}\frac{1}{4}\frac{1}{4}$ """ ??? $\frac{1}{4}\frac{1}{4}\frac{1}{4}$ """ ??? $\frac{1}{4}\frac{1}{4}\frac{1}{4}$ """ ???
$\frac{1}{4}\frac{1}{4}\frac{1}{4}$ """ ??? $\frac{1}{4}\frac{1}{4}\frac{1}{4}$ """ ??? $\frac{1}{4}\frac{1}{4}\frac{1}{4}$ """ ??? $\frac{1}{4}\frac{1}{4}\frac{1}{4}$ """ ???
j$\frac{1}{4}$j j"j j?j k$\frac{1}{4}$k k"k k?k l$\frac{1}{4}$l l"l l?l ;$\frac{1}{4}$; ;"; ;?;

Press the shift lock down for the next two lines.

$\frac{1}{4}\frac{1}{4}\frac{1}{4}$ """ ??? """ $\frac{1}{4}\frac{1}{4}\frac{1}{4}$??? $\frac{1}{4}\frac{1}{4}\frac{1}{4}$ """ ??? $\frac{1}{4}\frac{1}{4}\frac{1}{4}$ """ ???
""" $\frac{1}{4}\frac{1}{4}\frac{1}{4}$??? $\frac{1}{4}\frac{1}{4}\frac{1}{4}$ """ ??? $\frac{1}{4}\frac{1}{4}\frac{1}{4}$ """ ??? $\frac{1}{4}\frac{1}{4}\frac{1}{4}$??? """

USE THE KEYBOARD ILLUSTRATION TO LOCATE THE
SYMBOLS. DO NOT LOOK AT YOUR TYPEWRITER KEYS.

Repeat the practice exercises five times or
until you complete with no errors.

1) Proofread and circle all errors. Enter on
the chart below.

2) Note symbols repeatedly struck incorrectly
and practice again.

3) If more than two errors, repeat practice
exercise and evaluate yourself again.

SELF EVALUATION CHART
Lesson 16
(Electric Typewriters)

	!/1	@/2	#/3	$/4	%/5	¢/6	&/7	*/8	(/9	)/0	_/-	+/=
Top row												
1st evaluation												
2nd evaluation												
3rd evaluation												
2nd row from top												¼/½
1st evaluation												
2nd evaluation												
3rd evaluation												
Home key row												"/'
1st evaluation												
2nd evaluation												
3rd evaluation												
Bottom row												?//
1st evaluation												
2nd evaluation												
3rd evaluation												

LEARNING HOW TO TYPE

<u>Test your skill</u> (with symbols)

Tom said, "I want to go to the store. I have
50¢ to spend." Alice went along. The store was
called Mary & Sons Candy Shoppe. "May I help
you?" asked the owner. "Yes," answered Tom. I
would like 2 #3 sticks of licorice @ 4¢ and 6 #2
sticks @ 3¢. (That left the children 24¢ for
soda.) Tom drank ½ the soda. Alice drank only
¼ and saved the other ¼ to drink on the way home.

The senior class ordered rings. Some ordered
Style #2 and others ordered Style #4 (male/female).
There were no ½ sizes available. The rings were
ordered from Somerset & Company. The students
were given a 25% discount for ordering early.
The order form read: <u>ORDER MUST BE ACCOMPANIED
BY FULL PAYMENT OF $25.00.</u>* The girls' rings
had a light blue stone and the boys' rings had
a dark blue stone which was also larger in size
than the girls' stone.

*Make check payable to: SOMERSET & COMPANY

Repeat the above exercises five times. Proofread
and circle all errors. Note which letters are
repeatedly struck incorrectly and practice them

several times. When using the following charts to mark your errors, be sure to use the correct chart for your typewriter--electric or manual.

SELF EVALUATION CHART

(Manual Typewriter)

Top row	" /2	# /3	$ /4	% /5	— /6	& /7	' /8	(/9	) /0	* /-	+ /=		
1st evaluation													
2nd evaluation													
3rd evaluation													
2nd row from top	q	w	e	r	t	y	u	i	o	p	1/4	1/2	
1st evaluation													
2nd evaluation													
3rd evaluation													
Home key row	a	s	d	f	g	h	j	k	l	;	@ /¢		
1st evaluation													
2nd evaluation													
3rd evaluation													
Bottom row	z	x	c	v	b	n	m	,	.	? /			
1st evaluation													
2nd evaluation													
3rd evaluation													

LEARNING HOW TO TYPE

SELF EVALUATION CHART

(Electric Typewriter)

Top row	!/1	@/2	#/3	$/4	%/5	¢/6	&/7	*/8	(/9	)/0	−/-	+/=	
1st evaluation													
2nd evaluation													
3rd evaluation													

2nd row from top	q	w	e	r	t	y	u	i	o	p	¼/½		
1st evaluation													
2nd evaluation													
3rd evaluation													

Home key row	a	s	d	f	g	h	j	k	l	;	"/'		
1st evaluation													
2nd evaluation													
3rd evaluation													

Bottom row	z	x	c	v	b	n	m	,	.	?/			
1st evaluation													
2nd evaluation													
3rd evaluation													

HOW THE KEYBOARD WAS ARRANGED

Many beginning typists wonder why the keyboard is arranged   10
as it is instead of alphabetically. There are several good   20
reasons for this. First, letters are arranged to bring   30
those most frequently used directly under the operator's   40
hand. This is certainly more practical than having "a"   50
where "q" is, "t" where "z" is, etc. Second, letters are   60
arranged so that those most often used are struck by the   70
strongest fingers and with the easiest reaches. Imagine,   80
for example. how difficult it would be to have "e" where   90
"x" is. Third, letters are arranged so that you usually   100
use first one hand and then the other. As you have seen   110
even from the first lesson, your hands alternate during   120
typing. This alternating of the hands helps maintain that   130
rhythm which you will discover is so important in typing   140
well. Although there may be numerous ways of arranging   150
the keyboard for more efficient typing results, the present   160
location of the letters is easy to learn and permits the   170
average typist to attain a speed of sixty words per minute.   180
In fact, many have reached speeds of more than 100 words   190
per minute even on manual typewriters using the present   200
arrangement. This arrangement is certainly the best that   210
has been put on the market commercially and will most   220
probably be used without change for at least the next century.   230

	Words per minute	Number of errors
One-minute test		
1st evaluation	_____	_____
2nd evaluation	_____	_____
3rd evaluation	_____	_____
Three-minute test		
1st evaluation	_____	_____
2nd evaluation	_____	_____
3rd evaluation	_____	_____
Five-minute test		
1st evaluation	_____	_____
2nd evaluation	_____	_____
3rd evaluation	_____	_____

Lesson 17

TABULATOR

The tabulator is used to bring the carriage
to any point you set on your line of type. Tabulation stops are used to indent for paragraphs,
dates, salutations, block quotations or other
parts of a letter or typed text. Tabulation is
also used to set charts or tables into columns
or for setting up outlines for compositions,
reports, or other material to be developed.

How to set tab stops

Tabulation stops are set by moving the carriage or typing ball to the desired stop point
and pressing the tab set key. Pressing the tabulator bar will now move the carriage or typing
ball to any point set by the tab set key.

How to clear tab stops

Tabulation stops are cleared by tabulating to
the stop you wish to clear and pressing the tab
clear key.

To clear all stops in one easy motion, start
by moving the carriage or typing ball all the

way to the end of the page to the extreme right hand margin. Hold down the tab clear key. Using the carriage return on your typewriter, bring the carriage or typing ball back to the left hand margin. All stops will be cleared as the typewriter makes its way back to the left hand margin.

Setting tab stops for paragraph indentation

1) Clear all tab stops by using the above described method.

2) Make sure all tabs are clear by pressing the tabulator. If all tabs are clear, the carriage should go to the right hand margin with no stops in between. Clear any stops which remain by using your tab clear key.

3) Set your paragraph indentation for five spaces. To do this, bring the carriage or typing ball to the left hand margin, space five times and press the tab set key. Each time you hit the tabulator bar to indent for a paragraph, the carriage or typing ball will move to this spot automatically.

Practice exercises

Do these sentences to get the feel of using

the tabulator. Each time you hit the tab key,
return your fingers to the home keys. Some of
the sentences are alphabetic sentences, so you
will be getting some good keyboard practice too.
Repeat the exercise until you are using the tabulator key smoothly in your typing motions.

John and Mary wanted to go to the prom but it
was pouring rain and John's car did not have a
top. They took a cab.

Dick and Joan started a bee hobby. They
earned a lot of money selling honey.

Harriet and Mel started a fix-it shop. As
soon as they advertised, business started coming
in.

A quick brown fox slyly jumped over the lazy
dog three times before the dog awoke.

Pack a lunch box with six dozen sandwiches
to whet our appetites and quicken our step.

Jack would not have prized the exquisite
pigmy butterflies as Karen did.

The zeal of the brave boy won extra praise from the quick old judge.

The vexed proud squaw calmly juggled half a dozen milk bottles in the air.

The seemingly lazy horses gave a quick jerk which broke an axle and hurled the ambitious farmer upon his head.

He was puzzled to know how to coax the brave juggler to some quiet spot away from the brick platform, so that he could perform his trick to better advantage.

One of the bigger boys quickly threw the large javelin beyond the maximum distance and won the valuable prize.

The zealous student became quite exhausted and was dizzy before the journey through the park was half over.

The jury quickly agreed upon a verdict, and all except the musical zealot will be given a heavy fine.

Other indentations

Sometimes in a letter or report, you will have the usual paragraph indentation plus other material to be set off from the rest of the text. Some instances where this will occur are:

Letters will have indentations for:

a) paragraphs
b) date
c) complimentary closing
d) company name
e) writer's name
f) writer's title

Reports, term papers and other college material will have indentations for:

a) paragraphs
b) block quotations
c) sub-headings

Miscellaneous material such as brochures and programs will often have formats requiring different indentations for the various parts of the material to be typed or set up.

Lesson 18

IMPROVING YOUR SKILL

Now that you know the entire keyboard and have practiced use of the shift and tab keys, you will want to strengthen your confidence in typing and increase your speed. The following exercises will aid you in achieving these goals in various ways.

Some of the exercises are speed practice exercises to increase your speed. Other exercises deal with patterning your fingers to type the most frequently used words and phrases. This will increase both speed and accuracy. Practice all the exercises which follow to build your skill in both these areas.

For all exercises, use the following settings:

<u>Line Selector:</u> Set on 2 for double spacing

<u>Margins:</u> Pica - 10 and 70   Elite - 15 and 80

Speed practice

Type the entire following exercise once and check how long it takes. Repeat the exercise and check your second speed. Remember, speed is not as important as accuracy. Develop your speed slowly and steadily while you keep your accuracy at high levels at all times.

GETTING READY TO TYPE

When you are ready to begin typing, start by clearing 10
all margins. Then set the margins where you want them for 20
the material you are planning to type. Most times, your 30
margins will be set at 10 for the left and 70 for the right 40
hand margin. If it is to be straight typing, set your tab 50
stop at 5 for your paragraph indentation. After that, set 60
any other tab stops required in the text you are typing. 70

Once the margins and tabs are set, assume the proper 80
posture. If you are not sitting at a standard typewriter 90
table or desk, be sure to elevate your seat with a telephone 100
book or some other device to put you at the right height in 110
relation to the typewriter. This will prevent shoulder 120
fatigue. If you cannot set your feet on the floor, place 130
a small foot stool under the table where you are sitting. 140
You may find this stool useful even if you can reach the 150
floor with both feet. Many typists find it comfortable to 160
elevate one foot during long intervals of typing. This 170
prevents lower back pain and fatigue as it relieves the 180
strain on the lower back. 185

Have all your materials ready so that you will not have 195
to keep getting up and down. These include paper, carbon 205
paper, erasers or correcting materials, a copy stand, and 215
your copy material. By having everything ready before you 225
begin, you will not need to break your rhythm unnecessarily 235
by having to get up to get the items you need to work. 245

	Words typed	Minutes	Number of errors
1st evaluation	_____	_____	_____
2nd evaluation	_____	_____	_____
3rd evaluation	_____	_____	_____

Type the next five speed practice exercises using the time lengths indicated in the self-evaluation chart following each exercise.

SUGGESTIONS TO SPEED YOUR PROGRESS

Concentration means giving conscious attention to the   10
task that is being performed. Become oblivious to everything   20
except your typing. Keeping your eyes on the copy is most   30
important if you want to acquire speed and accuracy. Looking   40
back and forth from copy to machine and from machine to copy   50
causes a break in rhythm and a loss of time and speed.   60
Rhythm is a part of almost all our daily activities. In   70
typing, it means a uniform rate of typing over a period of   80
time--not slow and fast and fast and slow. Keep going.   90
Elimination of unnecessary motions is essential. Beginning   100
typists tend to move their hands up and down unnecessarily   110
each time a key is struck. Go immediately to the next key;   120
hold your hand over the guide keys--and keep on typing.   130

	Words per minute	Number of errors
One-minute test		
1st evaluation	_____	_____
2nd evaluation	_____	_____
3rd evaluation	_____	_____
Three-minute test		
1st evaluation	_____	_____
2nd evaluation	_____	_____
3rd evaluation	_____	_____

DEVELOP A TYPING HABIT

The only way to become better at typing is to use your   10
typewriter whenever you can. In the beginning, you may feel   20
as though you will never gain speed or strike every key without 30
stopping to think about where it is. All this will begin to   40
come to you naturally and automatically. Just be patient and 50
persevering, and practice a little each and every day.   60

For business people, typed correspondence is a must   70
for a professional image. Teachers prefer receiving typed   80
papers. Even personal letters written to corporations either 90
to praise, correct, or complain about a situation carry more 100
weight when they are typed. For all these reasons, whenever 110
you must put something down on paper, think about typing it. 120

As you begin to use your skill in all these ways, you   130
will become dissatisfied with handwritten reports, letters,   140
and bills. Your eye will prefer the neatness of type to   150
handwriting in many different circumstances. This alone will 160
spur you on to using your typing skill more and more. The   170
more typing you do, the easier and smoother it will become.   180

Five-minute test

	Words per minute	Number of errors
1st evaluation	_____	_____
2nd evaluation	_____	_____
3rd evaluation	_____	_____

<u>Speed practice</u>

Dear Tony,

The letter you are about to read has been typed by me,   10
myself and I alone. I am actually learning how to type.   20
That may surprise you. But I realized I would be needing it 30
when I start college next year so I decided to use part of   40
my summer vacation teaching myself how to type.   50

Yes, friend, you read right. I am learning how to type 60
from a book. Each day, I practice at least an hour. At   70
this point, I have learned all the keys, numbers, and   80
symbols. Now I am working on speed and accuracy. I do this 90
by testing myself over and over again. The more typing I do, 100
the faster I find myself going.   105

The system I am using is called the touch typing   115
method. That means you type by feel alone. You do not   125
look at the keys. At first, I didn't believe it would be   135
possible. But it is the weirdest thing. By using the   145
illustrations to learn where the keys were, my fingers   155
started to find them automatically. It really does make it 165
easier to copy what I am typing when I don't have to look   175
for the keys.

There are other things I'm doing this summer--swimming, 185
baseball, seeing girls--but I just wanted you to know I was 195
doing something really useful as well, for a change.   205

See you in the fall when I return from Pennsylvania.   215
Since we will be rooming together at school next year, I   225

think it would be in my best interest to present my typing   225
lesson book to you as a gift after I'm done with it.   If I   235
can learn this, anybody can.   240

                          Best regards,

                          Tom

                          Words per minute   Number of errors

One-minute test   _____   _____
Three-minute test   _____   _____
Five-minute test   _____   _____

<u>Speed practice</u>

FOR ALL YOUR TYPING NEEDS

Now that you have learned how to type, you will want	10
to know how to use your new skill. Throughout the remainder	20
of this book, you will find lessons in tabulating a chart	30
into evenly spaced columns, how to center horizontally and	40
vertically, how to place an address on an envelope or post	50
card, and even how to fold letters for different size envelopes.	60
You will also learn the format for typing different kinds	70
of letters, resumes, reports, outlines, manuscripts, and	80
college papers--even college papers with footnotes.	90
Just take each lesson as it comes. Follow instructions	100
step-by-step and use the forms as typing practice exercises.	110
This will accomplish two things at once: You will be improving	120
your typing skill; and you will be learning the forms you	130
need to know by actually setting them up and typing them out.	140
To complete your instruction, some lessons will deal	150
with typing aids, such as correction fluid and tape, carbon	160
paper, and many others. This will also include care of your	170
typewriter with instructions about cleaning fluids and methods.	180

	Words per minute	Number of errors
One-minute test		
1st evaluation	_____	_____
2nd evaluation	_____	_____
Three-minute test		
1st evaluation	_____	_____
2nd evaluation	_____	_____

CARE AND CLEANING OF YOUR TYPEWRITER

As you do more and more typing, you may begin to note   10

a difference in the neatness of the finished page. Some   20

of the open letters will appear to be filled in. This is   30

caused by bits of ribbon and ink which accumulate inside   40

the letters. This will happen to both standard typewriter   50

keys and typing balls. The problem is easily handled.   60

Many cleaning fluids are on the market. If none are   70

available, rubbing alcohol is a good substitute. Using a   80

swab, coat the heads of the key rods or the ball liberally   90

with the cleaning agent you have chosen. While still wet,   100

rub the letters gently with a soft toothbrush. Check the   110

cleaning job by striking each key in both upper and lower   120

case. If some keys are still shaded in, use a straight pin   130

to pick out any stubborn matter left behind by the toothbrush. 140

Repeat the test until every letter is perfectly sharp and   150

clean. Periodic cleaning of your keys in this manner will   160

prevent the problem before it occurs and will insure you   170

of producing neat work at all times.   180

After you have cleaned the keys, brush out all erasure   190

or correcting tape specks. Use a vacuum cleaner to draw   200

out stubborn pieces. Wipe the roller and all other parts   210

with a cloth moistened with alcohol to remove marks left   220

by carbon paper or other materials used with your typewriter. 230

Keep your typewriter covered when not in use. This will   240

prevent dust from settling on the exposed working parts and   250

will decrease the cleaning needs of your machine.   260

Five-minute test	Words per minute	Number of errors
1st evaluation	_____	_____
2nd evaluation	_____	_____
3rd evaluation	_____	_____

Patterning exercise

   To develop speed and accuracy, practice all
the following patterning exercises until your
fingers become familiar with all combinations.

COMMON PREFIXES

command commence commend commit common commune
commute compact comrade company compare compass
compel compete complain complex comply compute
computer companion

concern concept concise conclave conclude concur
concrete condemn condense condition contrition
conduction confection confer conference confess
confession

enable enact enclose encompass encore encroach
endanger endless endow endurance endure enforce
engage engender engrave engross engulf

exact exalt example excavate exceed excel except
excess exchange exclaim exclude excuse execute
exempt exercise exert exhale exit expense expect
expedite expel expend explain export expose

intercede intercept interchange interest interim
interlude interval interview intervene internal
international intermittent intermission intercom

probable probate problem procedure proceed
proclaim procure produce product profane profess
profile profit profound profuse program progress
prohibit prolong promise promote prompt propel
pronounce propose prosper protect

react rebate rebel rebound receive recipe recall
reclaim recognize recoil recommend record reduce
recount recourse recover recruit recur recurring
repeat redeem

subdivide subdue subject subjugate sublease
sublime submerge submit subscribe subsequent
subside subsist substance substitute subtract

underground undergrowth underline underneath
underpass understate underweight undercover
underhand undermine understand understudy
undertake

BLENDS

Blends consist of consonant and consonant-
vowel combinations and comprise two-thirds of
the elementary sounds of our language. They
occur about every third word. By practicing them,
you will increase your speed by patterning your
fingers. Th, pr and st are the most commonly

used blends but others are included here to complete the exercise. Practice each group five times or more.

th, pr, st

heath path bath health throw the thick the these this think thin
proud pray prince private prowl prize prove prime price
start state vest vast fast last stone stem stool store

wh, nk, ng, nch

whim whine whack wheel what where why whose when which
sank sink wink blink bank blank flank dank drank ankle
sang sing song long belong
wing fling cling wrong tong
cinch winch clinch bunch lunch crunch munch

qu, rt, ch, ct, rk

quite queer queen quote require quail quack quick
port pert sort fort snort heart dart tart mart start

child chicken children which witch bench inch
wench
elect verdict edict evict convict conduct attract
work fork cork ark mark park bark stork jerk
quirk

ld, lt, rd, mp, rl

hold held field bold gold told sold mold cold
weld
pelt belt bolt melt silt quilt built filter jilt
bard card cord board beard gourd word lard guard
lamp stamp vamp ramp camp damp dump limp cramp
curl earl enfurl Carl Charles marl burlap snarl

bl, cl, gl, pl, sl

blade blight blue blew bloom blossom blimp bland
climb climate cloth close cluster Clyde clutch
clue
glue glisten glove glum gloss glimpse glide glint
plate plaster plus plump plight plover plush
plume
slide slight sluice slush slope slip slime slip
slippery

sh, sk, sm, sn, sp, squ, sw

show shall should shoes lash rash shine shown shy
skit skip skate skein skin skim
ask mask task bask flask cask dusk musk tusk
small smith smell smoke smart smash smite smother
snow snail snake snag snob snoop snipe snug
snatch
spice span Spain spill spell spoke spool speak
asp raspy
squab squabble squad squadron squall square
squash squat
swam swim swan swain swish swear sweep sweet
swill

br, cr, gr, dr, fr, tr

broom bread brew bruise bruit brute brim brood
brisk
cry crate crave cruise crew crow crime cringe
cripple
grow grew grease grieve grave gross grass gripe
grip
drain drink drove driven drastic dram drip dread
drill
Fred friend afraid fracture fragile fragrant
train trod tramp trash trails tread trot trust

nt, nd, ly, ry, str, thr, spr, shr

went tent sent bent cent lent rent talent mantle
crescent
wend lend send land band sand hand brand find
hind rind
July rely nobly folly jolly
merry Perry dairy tarry hurry
strain stray strut strong strive strength stripe
straight
thread three thrust through thrill thrive thresh
threat
spry spring sprain spruce sprig spread sprang
sprite sprint
shred shrewd shriek shrill shrink shrine shrunk
shriven shrimp

oa, io, oi, lp

board boast roast toast hoard roar boar
notion action reaction eviction fiction diction
election
join joint loin coin moist joist hoist boil
boiler toil
help pulpit gulp pulp

In speech and in writing, some words show up
more frequently than others. The following
exercise lists the most frequently used words in
our language. For additional patterning, practice these words, repeating each group until you
can type all words smoothly.

1000 MOST USED WORDS

A

able aboard about above absence accept accident
according account across act action add addition
address adopt affair afraid after afternoon again
against age ago agreement air alike all allege
allow almost alone along already also although
always am among amount an and annual another
answer any anything anyway appear application
appoint appreciate April are argument army
around arrange arrangement arrest arrive article
as ask assist associate association assure at
athletic attempt attend attention August aunt
auto away automobile avenue await awful

B

baby back bad ball band bear be beautiful became
because become bed been before beg began begin

beginning begun behind believe belong beside
best better between big bill black block blow
blue board boat body book born both bought box
boy bridge bring broke brother brought build
built burn business busy but buy by

C

call came camp can cannot capture car card care
career carried carry case cast catch cause
celebration cent center century certain chain
change character charge check chief child
children Christmas church circular circumstance
cities citizen city claim class clean clear clerk
close clothing club cold collect colonies
combination come comfort coming command committee
common company complaint complete concern
condition conference connection consider
consideration contain convenience convict copy
cordially cost could country course court cover
crowd cut

D

dark dash date daughter day dead deal dear death
debate December decide decision declare deep
degree delay department desire destroy develop
diamond did died differ difference different

difficulty direct direction director disappoint
discussion distinguish distribute district do
divide doctor does dollar done don't door doubt
down dozen dress driven drown due during duty

E

each earliest early east easy eat education
effect effort eight either elaborate elect
election else emergency empire employ enclose
end engage engine enjoy enough enter entertain
entire entitle entrance escape especially estate
estimate even evening event ever every everything
evidence examination except exit expect expense
experience express extra extreme eye

F

face fact factory fail fair fall family famous
far farther father favor feature February feel
feet fell felt few field fifth fight figure file
fill final finally find fine finish fire firm
first five fix flight flower folks follow foot
for foreign forenoon forget form fortune forty
forward found four fourth free Friday friend
from front full further

G

game gave general gentlemen get getting girl
give glad glass go God goes gold gone good got
government grand grant great ground guess guest

H

had half hand happen happy hard has hat have he
heard hear head heart height held help her here
herself high him himself history hold home honor
hope horse hot hour house how however human hurt
husband

I

ice if illustrate immediate importance important
impossible imprison improvement in include income
increase indeed inform information injure inside
inspect instead intend interest into investigate
invitation is issue it itself

J

jail January judge judgment July June just
justice

K

keep kill kind knew know known knee

L

lady lake land large last late law lay lead
learn least leave led ledge left length less
lesson let letter liberty life light like line
list little live local long look lose loss lost
lot love low

M

machine madam made mail majority make man manner
many March marriage material matter May may
maybe mayor me mean meant measure meet member
men mention mere might mile mind mine minute
Miss miss Monday money month more morning most
mother motion mountain move Mr. Mrs. much must
my

N

name national navy near nearly necessary need
neighbor neither never new news newspaper next
nice night nine no none noon nor north not
nothing November now number

O

object objection oblige obtain occupy o'clock
October of off offer office official often old

omit on once one only open opinion or order
organization organize other ought our out
outside over own

P

page paid pair paper part particular party pass
past pay people perfect perhaps period person
personal picture piece place plan plant play
pleasant please pleasure point police political
poor popular population position possible post
pound power practical prefer preliminary prepare
present president press pretty price primary
principal principle print prison private probably
proceed progress promise prompt proper property
prove provide provision public publication
publish purpose push put

Q

question quiet quit quite quip quest quell

R

race railroad rain raise ran rapid rate rather
reach read ready real really reason receipt
receive recent recommend recover red refer
reference refuse regard region relative relief

remain remember repair reply report represent
request respectfully responsible rest restrain
result retire return ride right ring river road
room round royal rule run running

S

said sail salary same Saturday saw say says
scene school sea search second secretary section
secure see seem seen select Senate send sent
separate September serious serve service session
set seven several shall she shed ship short
should show shut sick side sight since sincerely
sir sister sit six size slide small so soap soft
sold some something sometimes son song soon
sorry south speak special spell spend spent
spring stamp stand start state statement station
stay steamer still stole stone stood stop stopped
story street struck study subject success such
sudden suffer suggest suit summer summon Sunday
supply support suppose sure surprise system

T

table take talk tax teach teacher tell ten tenth
term terrible testimony than thank that the
theater their them themselves then there
therefore these they thing think third this those

though thought three through throw Thursday thus
ticket time tire to today together told tomorrow
tonight too took top total toward town track
train travel treasurer tree trip trouble true
truly trust try Tuesday turn two

U

unable uncle under understand unfortunate unless
until up upon us use usual

V

vacation various very vessel victim view visit
visitor volume vote veto

W

wait walk want warm was watch water way we wear
weather Wednesday week weight well went were
west what when where whether which while white
who whole whom whose why wife will wind winter
wire wish with within without witness woman
women wonder wonderful word work world worth
would wreck write written wrote

Y

yard year yes yesterday yet you young your

Z

zero zip zipper zest zealous zealot

Lesson 19

HORIZONTAL CENTERING

Horizontal centering means typing a title or other material so that half the number of letters are on each side of the center of the page. To do this, follow these three steps:

1) Find the center of your page. Make a vertical center fold in a sheet of paper $8\frac{1}{2}$ x 11 inches. Open the page flat and insert it into your typewriter. Space to the center fold and press your tab set key.

2) Always tabulate to the center of the paper when getting ready to center horizontally.

3) Backspace one space for every two letters, spaces, or marks in the title. Do not backspace for an odd letter or mark at the end. An easy way to do this is to spell the title out loud, depressing the back-space key on every other letter, space, or mark that you sound out.

O I O T L C N E I G
H R Z N A E T R N
spacel

In sounding out the title "Horizontal Centering," depress the back-space key for each stroke that appears above the line. Sounding out titles in this manner establishes an easy rhythm which you will use every time you center.

When you type the title in, it should look
like this--perfectly centered:

HORIZONTAL CENTERING

Practice exercise

Using the method described above, center each
of the following items:

Your own name
Locust School Spring Program
New Jersey Tax Schedule
Class of 1984 Graduation Program
History of the Reformation
The Spanish Inquisition
The Psychology of Learning How to Succeed

Lesson 20

VERTICAL SPACING

Vertical spacing means placing
titles or other material neatly
spaced vertically on the page.
This is used in title pages for
college papers, manuscripts and
other material requiring a title
page.

Vertical spacing is also used
for centering poems or other short
works vertically on a page so that
the top and bottom spaces are pro-
portionately divided to present a
neat appearance.

Before you begin your lesson in
vertical spacing, you should be
aware that 8½ x 11-inch paper contains 66 single spaces from top to
bottom and 8½ x 14-inch paper
(commonly called legal size) contains 74 spaces. At the right is
a numbered Vertical Guide Strip
used for vertical spacing. You

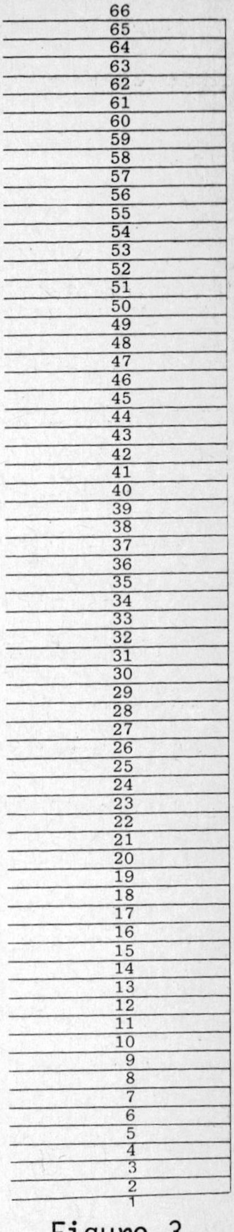

Figure 3.
Vertical
guide strip

can make one of your own by following the easy instructions below.

Use your guide strip for centering titles or any other material in vertical placement on the page. When you decide where such material goes vertically, center it horizontally, using the method described for horizontal centering.

Insert Vertical Guide Strip in your typewriter side by side with paper as illustrated. Hold in place with paper bail to keep from slipping.

How to Make a Vertical Guide Strip

1) Roll a sheet of paper into your typewriter until just the tip of the top edge comes through.

2) Space down one line and, starting at the left edge, type a solid line about 2 inches long.

3) Continue spacing down one line at a time all the way to the bottom, typing a solid line on each space.

4) Put the paper back into your typewriter and type the number 66 above the top line. Counting backward, number each line in the same way until you reach number 1 at the bottom.

5) Cut the strip off. (Be sure to make your strip from paper. Anything heavier will cause the sheet you're typing on to slip.)

6) Insert the strip into your typewriter side by side with your page, making sure the top edges of both are lined up. The strip will indicate how many lines are left on the page at any given point. (See Fig. 3, p. 131)

When working on legal-size paper, 8½ x 14 inches, if you wish to make a Vertical Guide Strip to aid you in judging the length of your page, use the same instructions as above on the larger sheet of paper, but begin the top line with number 74.

Because these Vertical Guide Strips tend to wear out with heavy use, you may wish to make several at one time or make one and have several photocopies made in order to have extras on hand as needed.

Practice exercise

Try the following title pages and program covers one at a time. If you make mistakes in centering, either vertically or horizontally, just pull the page out and start over. The most important discovery you will make is that you can produce a title page or any similar material neatly and properly spaced.

In setting these pages up, follow these two simple steps:

1) Decide where each line is to go in vertical placement on the page. Note these line numbers on your copy. Insert the paper and the Vertical Guide Strip into your typewriter.

2) As you bring your page to the line desired, center the line horizontally before typing. Type the line, then move down to the next line in the copy.

GONE WITH THE WIND	Union College •
by	Women in Literature
Margaret Mitchell	by Nicole Monteret
(See Fig. 10, p. 181)	Literature 202
	Prof. Mary Moore
	January 5, 1984
	(See Fig. 11, p. 182)

After you have successfully set up the above exercises, try the two exercises which follow. In these exercises, some of the titles are too long to be placed on one line. For better appearance, break the long titles up into two

lines, making the second line shorter than the
first line of the title.   (See Fig. 12, p. 183.)

Union College

A Comparison of Women in the Works of
Anton Chekhov and Henrik Ibsen

by Nicole Monteret

Literature 203

Prof. Mary Moore

January 5,]984

Kean College

Effects of Fear of Success in
Women of the 1980s

by Joan Laslow

Psychology 102

Professor Andrea Klaus

June 6, 1984

Lesson 21

TABULATIONS

In Lesson 17, you learned how to set tab
stops to indent for paragraphs and other indented
material in straight typing or outlines. This
lesson will demonstrate the use of tabulation in
setting up charts and tables into evenly spaced
columns. Just follow the steps one at a time
and you will learn to set up tabulations in two,
three, four, and five columns with ease.

Calculating tab stops for evenly spaced columns

1) Add up the number of letters and spaces in
the longest entry in each column.

2) Multiply the number of columns minus 1 by
6 spaces (which you will leave between columns).

3) Total the answers from Steps #1 and #2.

4) Divide by 2.

5) Begin at the center of your page and back-
space the answer from Step #4. This sets the
margin or tab stop for your first column.

6) Tap out the spaces in the longest entry in
the first column. Then tap out the six spaces
to be left between columns. Press the tab stop

LEARNING HOW TO TYPE

for your second column. Repeat Step #6 until
all tabs are set.

Following the six steps above, set up the
following tabulations. Each practice exercise
includes a full explanation for setting up the
chart and may be used for pica or elite without
change.

Two-column tabulation

ADULT EDUCATION CLASSES

Touch Typing	Monday & Tuesday
Wood Finishing	Monday & Tuesday
Tennis I	Monday & Tuesday
Tennis II	Tuesday & Wednesday

Longest entry in each column	Number of spaces
Wood Finishing	14
Tuesday & Wednesday	19
Total	33
Number of columns minus 1 times 6	6
Total	39
Divide by 2 39 ÷ 2 = 19 (drop fractions)	

Type the tabulation as follows:

1) Center the title

2) Drop down two lines

3) Backspace 19 spaces

4) Set the left hand margin to begin the first column.

5) Tap out the number of spaces in the longest entry plus the 6 spaces to be left between columns. Set the tab stop for the second column.

Your tabulation should look like this.

ADULT EDUCATION CLASSES

Touch Typing	Monday & Tuesday
Wood Finishing	Monday & Tuesday
Tennis I	Monday & Tuesday
Tennis II	Tuesday & Wednesday

ADULT EDUCATION CLASSES

Touch Typing	Monday & Tuesday	7-8 P.M.
Wood Finishing	Monday & Tuesday	7-9 P.M.
Tennis I	Monday & Tuesday	7:30-9:00 P.M.
Tennis II	Tuesday & Wednesday	6-8:30 P.M.

Longest entry in each column	Number of spaces
Wood Finishing	14
Tuesday & Wednesday	19
7:30-9:00 P.M.	14
Total	47
Number of columns minus 1 times 6 spaces	12
Total	59

Divide by 2   59 ÷ 2 = 29 (drop fractions)

Type the tabulation as follows:

1) Center the title

2) Drop down two lines

3) Backspace 29 spaces

4) Set the left hand margin for the first column.

5) Tap out the number of spaces in the longest

entry in the first column plus the 6 spaces to
be left between columns. Set the tab stop for
the second column.

6) Tap out the number of spaces in the longest entry in the second column plus 6 spaces to
be left between columns. Set the tab stop for
the third column.

7) If tabulation has more than three columns,
repeat steps 5 and 6 for additional columns.

Your three-column tabulation should look like
this:

ADULT EDUCATION CLASSES

Touch Typing	Monday & Tuesday	7-8 P.M.
Wood Finishing	Monday & Tuesday	7-9 P.M.
Tennis I	Monday & Tuesday	7:30-9:00 P.M.
Tennis II	Tuesday & Wednesday	6-8:30 P.M.

Tabulations with column heads

When setting up a tabulation with column
heads, plan the columns exactly as you would
without heads. If any column head is the longest entry in that column, use it to figure the

number of spaces to be left for that column. Try
this exercise with column heads added.

ADULT EDUCATION CLASSES

<u>Course</u>	<u>Days</u>	<u>Time</u>
Touch Typing	Monday & Tuesday	7-8 P.M.
Wood Finishing	Monday & Tuesday	7-9 P.M.
Tennis I	Monday & Tuesday	6:30-9:30 P.M.
Tennis II	Tuesday & Wednesday	6-8:30 P.M.

Practice exercise

Using the method demonstrated above, practice the following tabulations.

MIDDLE SCHOOL HONOR ROLL LIST (to be centered) 3-column tabulation

5th grade	6th grade	7th grade
Mary Simms	Kelly Thompson	Gerard Brown
Thomas Melvin	Andrea Greenville	Elena Venezia
Karen Mary Jackson	Linda Buxton	Catherine Elliott
Morgan Johnson	John Burnside	Melanie Francois
Harold Santucci	Joseph Rowland	Jessie Wilkinson

9TH GRADE ELECTIVE SUBJECTS (to be centered) 3-column tabulation

Languages	Literature	History
Latin	Women in Literature	English History I
Spanish	Shakespeare Survey	Russian History I
French	English Literature I	Western Civilization I
Italian	Irish Literature	Greek History
German	Introduction to Drama	Early American History

MENU SELECTIONS (to be centered) 4-column tabulation

Meats	Vegetables	Fruit	Dessert
Sirloin Steak	Carrots	Apple	Ice Cream
Veal cutlet	Green beans	Plum	Cheesecake
Chicken	Broccoli	Grapefruit	Sherbet
Hamburger	Potatoes	Peach	Chocolate Cake
Pork Chops	Tomatoes	Grapes	Rice Pudding
Lamb Chops	Lettuce	Orange	Jell-o

INVENTORY - JUNE 1983 (to be centered) 5-column tabulation

Item	Color	Size	Price	Pieces in stock
Sweater	Pink	12	$5.99	1 dozen
Sweater	Orange	12	$5.99	½ dozen
Dress	Pink stripe	14	$9.99	7
Dress	Blue stripe	12	$9.99	8
Skirt	Black pleated	10	$7.89	10

3

More About Your Typewriter

Once you have learned how to type, you will begin to find other techniques necessary to get the most out of your typewriter. In some cases, this will simply mean learning all the time saving features on your particular machine and how to use them. In other cases, it will mean learning how to extend the actual capabilities of your machine to assist you in various situations such as letter omissions and other typing problems. Each of these will be demonstrated with practice exercises to illustrate the solution.

Squeezing in omitted letters

Please carr the ball to the field.

Squeeze by moving the
carriage to the space
between the word with
the missing letter and
the following word.
Backspace a half space
and squeeze the missing
letter against the last
typed letter in the
incomplete word. If
your typewriter cannot
backspace a half space,
push the carriage slightly
to the right to squeeze
the missing letter onto
the end of the incomplete
word.

Example

Please carry the ball to the field.

OR

Please carr the ball to the field.

Erase the entire word.
Move to the 1st space of
the erased word. Backspace
a half space and type the
word, backspacing a half
space for each letter,
thereby centering the five-
letter word in the four-
letter spot by cutting down
the size of the space between
the words before and after
the newly squeezed word.

Example

Please carry the ball to the field

Spreading a word

We lives in New York.

Erase the entire word.
Move to the second letter
space in the erased word.
Backspace a half space and
type the first letter of
the erased word. Backspace
one half space for each
letter until the entire word
is typed. This centers the
shorter word between the
words before and after the
newly typed word.

Example

We l i v e in New York.

Word alignment

We ^{live}in New York.

Turn roller up to lower.

We _{live} in New York.

Turn roller down to raise.

To test your position when
attempting to align a word
with the rest of the
sentence, set your typewriter
on stencil and strike the
first letter of the word to
to be inserted. Check the
impression for proper
positioning and make adjustments
as necessary.

Justifying the right hand margin

Sometimes you will want the
right hand margin to be
completely even. This is
done by spreading out some
words and using the half
space to squeeze other words
in so that the right margin
ends evenly.

Sometimes you will want the
r i g h t h a n d margin to be
completely e v e n . This is
done by spreading o u t some
words and using t h e h a l f
space to squeeze other words
in so that the right margin
ends evenly.

Ending one line evenly with another

Example

        John Hamilton
         President

Type the first line and go
down in the same space (one
space after the last letter
in the first line) to the
next line. Backspace the
number of spaces and letters
to be typed in the second
line. Type in the title or
other material to be lined
up in the right hand margin
with the line above as in
the example at the left.

How to make symbols not included on the keyboard

Minus sign	–	Strike the dash. Leave one space before and after the minus sign.
Plus or addition sign	+	Strike the dash. Backspace once. Turn roller slightly up and strike apostrophe. Leave one space before and after plus sign.
Division sign	÷	Strike the colon. Backspace once. Strike the dash. Space once before and after a division sign.
Multiplication sign	x	Strike small x. Leave one space before and after multiplication sign.
Equal sign	=	Turn roller slightly up. Strike dash. Backspace once. Turn roller slightly down. Strike dash. Leave one space before and after equal sign.
Degree (85°)	o	Type number. Turn roller down slightly and hit small o.
Exponents	3^{2}	Type the first number. Turn roller down slightly. Type exponent. No space between numbers.
Chemical symbols	$H_{2}O$	Type letter. Turn roller slightly up and type number. Bring roller back to original position and type remaining letters. No spaces between letters and numbers.
Fractions not on keyboard	2-3/4 7/8	Use slash and dash where needed.

Feet and inches	'	Apostrophe for feet
	"	Quotation marks for inches
(12'4" = 12 ft. 4 in.)		(when expressed in numbers)
Hours and minutes	'	Apostrophe for hours
	"	Quotation marks for minutes
(4'3" = 4 hrs. 3 min.)		(when expressed in numbers)
Ditto marks	"	Use quotation marks.
Exclamation point	!	Strike the period.
		Backspace once.
		Strike apostrophe.
Long dash	--	Use a double hyphen with
		no space before or after.
(Typing is a skill which		
can be learned--not an		
inborn talent.)		
Footnote numbers		Turn roller slightly down.
		Type footnote number with
They won the game.[2]		no space between word and
		number.
Caret	_/	Underscore last letter
		before insert.
ball		Strike slash.
They went to th_e/park.		Turn roller down slightly
		and type insert.
Brackets	_[_]	Left Bracket:
		Hit slash.
		Backspace a half space.
		Hit underscore.
		Turn roller down one full
		space.
		Backspace once.
		Hit underscore.
		Right Bracket:
		Hit underscore
		Hit slash.
		Turn roller down one full
		space.
		Backspace 1½ spaces.
		Hit underscore.

Erasing on the typewriter

Roll the paper up in your typewriter until you are clear of the ribbon carrier. Bring your carriage to the extreme right or left so that specks from your eraser will not fall into the typewriter.

If erasing carbon copies, place a piece of light cardboard or other shield behind each copy when you erase to prevent a smudge from being rubbed onto the next copy by pressure from erasing on the carbon paper.

Note: For more on corrections, see page 230.

Making carbon copies

Most people make a carbon copy of important letters or papers when the original cannot be retained for any reason. The carbon copy is usually made of a lower grade of paper called a second sheet.

When setting up for one or more carbon copies, follow these easy steps:

1) Place the second sheet down flat

on your desk.

2) Place a sheet of carbon paper inked side down on the second sheet.

3) If making only one copy, place the original on top of the carbon paper. If making more carbon copies, follow with another second sheet and another sheet of carbon, inked side down, until you have the number of copies required. End with the original on top.

4) Pick up the set and make sure all edges are even. Keep the inked side of the carbon paper facing you when you even up the edges.

5) Roll the papers into the type-writer. Be sure that the dull side of the carbon paper is on top facing you when the sheets are in the typewriter and that the shiny inked side is facing away from you for typing. Straighten the edges and start typing.

4

General Typing Information

Punctuation on the typewriter

Period (.)   Leave two spaces after
                     a period ending a sen-
                     tence.

Question mark (?) Leave two spaces after
                     a question mark.

Exclamation point (!) Leave two spaces after
                     an exclamation point.

Colon (:)   Leave two spaces after
                     a colon.

Quotation marks (") Leave two spaces after
                     quotation marks ending
                     a quote.

Comma (,)   Leave one space after
                     a comma.

Semicolon (;)   Leave one space after
                     a semicolon.

Parentheses ( )
(two children)

Leave no space after opening parentheses and no space between the last word before closing parentheses.

Dash (-)

Leave no space before or after when a dash is used to hyphenate or divide a word.

Double dash (--)

No space before or after a double or long dash.

Asterisk (*)

No space between the last word and asterisk or between asterisk and first word of reference.

Ellipsis (...)

When used in the middle of the sentence, leave a space before and after; when used to begin a sentence, leave no space after; when used to complete a sentence, leave two spaces after ellipsis.

Setting up quotation marks and parentheses

When a period or question mark ends a complete thought to be enclosed within parentheses or within quotation marks, it should be typed this way:

The morning is hazy. *2 spaces* (It was supposed

to rain.) *2 spaces* The picnic will be held anyway.

The morning is hazy *one space* (with predictions

of rain threatening), *one space* but we will hold

the picnic anyway.

The morning is hazy *one space* (no rain, please

God) *one space* so we will hold the picnic anyway.

Quotation marks, periods, and question
marks for complete, unbroken quotes:

    Tina asked, *one space* "May I come with you?"

Mary answered,ʌ "If you have finished

cleaning your room."

Quotation marks, commas, and periods when
the quote is broken or separated into
two parts:

"I have been away for so long,"ʌ Tina

exclaimed,ʌ "but now I'm home for good."

Meaning of special characters and symbols

Quotation mark   (")   Quotations, ditto, inches, and seconds with numbers.

12'4" = 12 feet 4 inches or 12 hours 4 minutes.

Number sign   (#)   Means number when placed before a figure and pounds after a figure

#4 = number 4
4# = 4 pounds

Dollar sign   ($)   Used with figures

Percent sign   (%)   Used in tabulations or charts but is usually avoided in formal writing.

Underscore   (_)   Used for underlining or for making an unbroken horizontal line. Titles of books, periodicals, newspapers, and songs are underlined. Italics are indicated by underlining the word or words to be italicized. Foreign words or phrases are underlined in formal writing.

Ampersand (&)	Used only in tabulations and with the names of firms. It should not be used to indicate the word "and" in formal writing.
Apostrophe (')	Used for apostrophe, feet and minutes with numbers, or when indicating a quote within a quote.
	Mary said, "Tom, did you hear Frank say, 'Mary, mind your manners,' when he visited us yesterday?"
Parentheses ( )	Used for explanatory phrases, and chemical compounds.
Asterisk (*)	Used for footnotes and sometimes as a device for calling special attention to tabular entries.
Cent sign (¢)	Used with figures to indicate money value.
At sign (@)	Used with figures to indicate money value.

Slash (/)   Used for typing
                         fractions not on
                         the keyboard, dates,
                         as a caret for in-
                         sertions in typed
                         matter, and in spe-
                         cial situations such
                         as and/or, he/she.

Hyphen   (-)   Used in compounds
                         or hyphenated words.
                         It is also used in
                         typing mixed numbers
                         such as 1-3/4.
                            In typing, a double
                         dash (--) is used to
                         indicate a printer's
                         long dash.

NUMBERS

How to express numbers in words

Words below one hundred are hyphenated when written out but hundreds and thousands are not hyphenated.

Examples

twenty-six	one hundred twenty-six
sixty-two	one thousand two hundred sixty-two
eighty-five	eighteen thousand one hundred eighty-five

Write numbers out in words when:

The number is the first word in a sentence.	One man stopped the train.
Writing a street or avenue in numbers under ten except with east, west, north or south.	15 West 5th Street 352 Second Avenue
The house number is 1.	One Chatterley Lane
The number is part of a proper noun.	The Sixth Symphony

Time of day used with o'clock.	I met him at four o'clock.
Fractions appear alone in text.	Only three-fourths of the class attended.
Numbers used in the body of the text.	Tom and Jane are married seven years.
Approximate sums of money are given.	Jean spent about fifty dollars.
Approximate ages are given.	Many women around forty start new careers.
Numbers in text are below ten.	She went to school for eight years.
Round numbers are used.	They asked seventy children to go to the circus.
Ordinals are used in a sentence.	This is the fourth time that house was sold.

Write numbers as figures when:

Preceded by a noun.	Starfleet 6 Order No. 24
Expressed as percent or decimal in text.	6 percent 1.2 percent

Used with a symbol.	#4 7% $42 5¢
Using house numbers except One.	422 Barns Street One Park Avenue
Listing weights, dimensions, distances, or degrees.	5 lbs. 72 miles 8° 16 x 14
Citing numbers above 10.	They had 17 cups.
Writing street name above 10.	Mary lives at 123 West 11th Street
Numbers or fractions in a series.	The teacher bought 6 notebooks, 7 pencils, and 3 erasers.
Time used with a.m. and p.m.	11:30 p.m.
Special dates or eras.	The 18th Century The Class of '82 The Roaring 20's
Exact age in years, months, and days.	2 years, 8 months, 7 days
Writing sums of money in round numbers. Use no ciphers.	They paid $1,278 for the wagon. They spent $62 for dinner.
When writing two numbers together, express the larger number in figures.	The teacher bought 6 three-cent pencils.

Roman numerals on the typewriter

Use capital letters except for front matter in a manuscript (title page, table of contents, etc.). Capital "i" is used for 1.

1	I	6	VI	50	L
2	II	7	VII	100	C
3	III	8	VIII	500	D
4	IV	9	IX	1,000	M
5	V	10	X		

A repeated letter repeats the value:

III = 3　　　　XX = 20　CCC = 300

A letter occurring after one of greater value is added:

VI = 6　　　　LV = 55　MC = 1,100

A letter occurring before one of greater value is subtracted:

XL = 40　　　　IX = 9　CM = 900

A dash over a numeral multiplies it by 1,000:

$\overline{L}$ = 50,000　$\overline{C}$ = 100,000　$\overline{DLVI}$ = 556,000

Use of Roman numerals

1) To designate the most important divisions of a composition--not the sub-divisions.

2) No period is used after Roman numerals except when used in headings in accordance with the general punctuation.

Henry VIII   George III   Elizabeth I

3) If two sets are used, distinguish by writing one set in lower case:

i = 1   ii = 2   x = 10   xi = 11

This form is used for the frontispiece and all other pages preceding the first page of a book or manuscript.

4) When typing a series of Roman numerals, leave two spaces after each for easy reading.

Chapters I, II, III, and IV deal with books.

PROOFREADER'S MARKS USED IN EDITING

⤳   Apostrophe or single quotation mark

‿   Close up (basket ball)

৲   Comma

⤶   Delete

stet   Let it stand (do not delete even though crossed out)

∧   Insert

¶   Begin a new paragraph

No ¶   Do not begin a new paragraph.
              run in

⊙   Period

⤳ ⤳   Double quotation marks

Leave more space

∽   Transpose elements, usually with "tr" in margin

     (their)   or   ((in margin))

◯   Reverse form (change (five) to 5 and (rt.) to right)

/   Slash through capital letter means use lower case. (T = t)

≡   Capital letter (d = D)

⅂ ⌐   Put in center of page   ⅂ My Song ⌐

_____   Set in italics

Edited copy

The main purpose of this book is to ~~get you...~~ *teach* s̶

~~about the business of learning~~ how to type.
If you do a new
~~Taking each~~ lesson ~~as it comes~~ *each day—* and giv~~es~~ *ing* it
at least
one full hour ~~everyday~~ will ~~have you~~ *you be touch* typing in

less than ~~one~~ *a* month. ~~But~~ if that pace is too

fast for you, ~~then slow down~~ *relax.* ~~This is strictly~~ *You're not in*

a race.
~~a self taught course~~. ~~You are in full control~~.

~~Remember~~ you are teaching yourself a valuable

skill which is becoming more and more important
many, many
in the everyday lives of ~~everyday~~ people and you
your typing skills for
will find uses for ~~it~~ the rest of your life, so
whatever *you need to*
take ~~your~~ time and learn them well.

<u>Corrected copy</u>

The main purpose of this book is to teach you how to type. If you do a new lesson each day--giving it at least one full hour--you will be touch typing in less than a month. If that pace is too fast for you, relax. You're not in a race. You are teaching yourself a valuable skill which is becoming more and more important in the everyday lives of many, many people. You will find uses for your typing skills for the rest of your life, so take whatever time you need to learn them well.

FORMS OF ADDRESSES AND SALUTATIONS

Title	Envelope and Inside Address	Salutation	Complimentary Close
The President	The President The White House Washington, D.C.	Sir or Madam: Mr./Madam President: Dear Mr. President: Dear Madam President: My dear Mr. President: My dear Madam President:	Very truly yours,
United States Senator	The Honorable........... The United States Senate Washington, D.C.	Sir or Madam: Dear Sir or Madam: My dear Senator: Dear Senator........: My dear Senator......:	Very truly yours,
Governor	His/Her Excellency the Governor Capital City, State Zip or The Honorable........... Governor of.......... Capital City, State Zip	Sir or Madam: Dear Sir or Madam: Dear Governor........:	Very truly yours,
Mayor	His/Her Honor the Mayor City, State Zip or The Honorable.......... Mayor of the City of...... City, State Zip	Dear Sir or Madam: Dear Mayor..........: My dear Mayor........:	Very truly yours,
Judge	The Honorable.......... Judge of the Superior Court City, State Zip	Sir or Madam: Dear Judge...........:	Very truly yours,
General or Admiral	General.............. Department of National Defense Washington, D.C. Admiral.............. (as above)	Sir or Madam: Dear Sir or Madam: My dear Sir: My dear Madam: Dear General.........: Dear Admiral.........:	Very truly yours,

Title	Envelope and Inside Address	Salutation	Complimentary Close
The Pope	His/Her Holiness Pope............ Vatican City, Italy	Your Holiness:	Respectfully yours,
Bishop (Protestant or Catholic)	The Right Reverend Bishop of......... City, State Zip	Right Reverend Sir: Right Reverend Madam: Your Excellency: Dear Bishop.........:	Respectfully yours,
Priest (Secular)	The Rev. ....Church City, State Zip	Dear Reverend.......:	Respectfully yours,
Brother	Brother........... Street address City, State Zip	Dear Brother: Dear Brother........:	Respectfully yours,
Sister	Sister........... Street Address City, State Zip	Dear Sister: Dear Sister........:	Respectfully yours,
Mother Superior	Mother............ Name of Convent Street address City, State Zip	Dear Mother Superior:	Respectfully yours,
Rabbi	Rev. or Rabbi....... Temple............. Street address City, State Zip	Reverend Sir: Reverend Madam: Dear Rabbi:	Respectfully yours,
Business	Name of Company Street address City, State Zip	Dear Manager: Dear Associate: Dear Mr.......: Dear Mrs......: Dear Miss.....: Dear Ms.......:	Very truly yours, Sincerely yours,

5

Basic Forms for School, Business and Personal Use

LETTERS

For business people, a typed letter is a must, but you will find many personal uses for typed letters too. Some of these instances might be when submitting a resume or applying for a job.

After content, setup is of prime importance in a letter. With practice, you will be able to set up your own neatly typed business letters.

Business letters

Most letters are typed single spaced with margins set at 10 and 70. If the text is short and you are using a full

8½ x 11-inch sheet of paper, you can still produce an attractive letter by changing your right and left margins to suit the setup. Start by resetting your margins at 15 and 65. If the letter is really short, you may even go to settings of 20 and 60. The important effect to achieve is a neatly typed, well balanced arrangement on the page.

Figures 4 and 5 illustrate two basic business letter formats which will cover most situations. Use these samples to set up the practice letters which follow.

Letter practice exercise

January 5, 1983/The Franklin State Bank/ 1424 West Street/Union, New York 11201/ Attention: Mrs. Elena Marsh, President/ Dear Mrs. Marsh: This is to inform you that I am closing my savings and checking accounts in your bank. The reason for this is that I am moving my business to another state. As you have no branch in my new location, I must move my account to a more convenient banking institution.

LETTERHEAD

Date

2 spaces — Addressee's Name
Street
City, State Zip   (all words spelled out—no abbreviations)

2 spaces — Attention: (or Re:)

2 spaces — Salutation:

Paragraphs indented 5 or 10 spaces.........................
....
....

3 spaces — Body single-spaced—2 spaces between paragraphs............
....
....

2 spaces — ....
....
....

Complimentary close,

COMPANY NAME   (in solid capitals)   2 spaces

(Writer's signature)   4 spaces

(leave 4 single spaces for
signature)

no space — Initials
(Writer/Typist)
2 spaces — Enc. (If any enclosures with letter)   Writer's name typed
Title (if used)
cc: (If carbon copies going to
anyone with names and
addresses noted)

Figure 4. Sample letter - modified block style

```
                              LETTERHEAD



              Date




              Addressee's Name
              Address
              City, State Zip    (all words spelled out--no abbreviations)
  2 spaces
              Attention:  (or Re:)
  2 spaces
              Salutation:
  2 spaces
              Paragraphs are not indented in solid block style.  Everything is
              started at the left hand margin.  Sometimes this form is used in
              the body with only the date, complimentary close and signature
              indented just past the center.
  2 spaces
              Body single-spaced--2 spaces between paragraphs.................
              .............................................................
              .............................................................
              .............................................................
  2 spaces
              .............................................................
              .............................................................
  2 spaces
              Complimentary close,
  2 spaces
              COMPANY NAME    (in solid capitals)
  2 spaces
              (Writer's signature)
  4 spaces
              Writer's Name typed
              Title (if used)
  2 spaces
             ⌜Initials
  no space   ⎜(Writer/Typist)
             ⌞Enc.  (if any enclosures with letter)
  2 spaces
              cc:  (if carbon copies going to anyone with
                    names and addresses entered, if requested)
```

Figure 5.   Sample letter - block style

I have been pleased with your service to me during the years I have lived and worked in Union and would certainly recommend it to any of my friends, relatives or business associates.

Thank you for your assistance over the years.
Very truly yours/Edmundson's Department Store/John Edmundson/Proprietor

January 5, 1983/Mr. John Miller/911 Butin Street/Jefferson City, Missouri/ Dear Mr. Miller: Thank you for informing us that you have not received the equipment which you ordered through our former representative, Mr. B.C. Owens.

It is necessary that we have your copy of the order blank as requested in our telegram because this paper contains a complete record of the transaction and will enable us to take the proper action without further delay. It seems that the original order blank forwarded to us by Mr. Owens has been lost as it never reached us.

We regret any inconvenience this may
cause you and look forward to receiving
your copy of the order blank so that your
equipment can be delivered to you without
any further delay.
Yours truly/National Utilities, Inc./
Janet C. Burnside, Sales Representative

September 23, 1982/Professor John Clayes/
142 Elliott Street/Brooklyn, New York
11225/Dear Professor Clayes: Our
University Book Club has a novel plan of
book selection and reading.   About fifty
books are selected, by vote of club members,
bers, from a list of five hundred titles,
and circulated in groups of three and
four, from the beginning to the end of
each academic year.   Each group is retained for two weeks and then passed on
to another member.

Since this is your first year with us,
we are enclosing an application for a
membership card.   If you wish to join

the Club this year, please sign the application and return it by October 5. Sincerely yours/Dr. Ann Sheridan

Personal letters

When typing personal letters on stationery bearing no letterhead as in Figures 6 and 7, the inside address must be typed. There are two ways to set this up:

1) Type the street address, city and state, and the date in three lines in block formation at the top of the page in line with the complimentary closing. (See Figure 6.)

2) Type the date at the top properly spaced and lined up with the complimentary closing. Add the street address, city, and state with zip code at the bottom lined up with and immediately following your name in block form. (See Figure 7.)

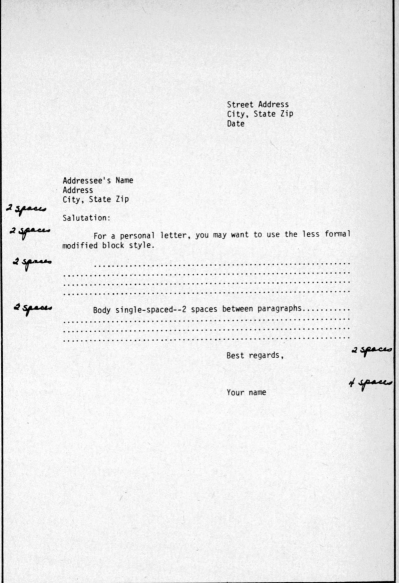

```
                              Street Address
                              City, State Zip
                              Date



        Addressee's Name
        Address
        City, State Zip

        Salutation:

              For a personal letter, you may want to use the less formal
        modified block style.

              .................................................
              .................................................
              .................................................
              .................................................

              Body single-spaced--2 spaces between paragraphs...........
              .................................................
              .................................................
              .................................................

                              Best regards,


                              Your name
```

2 spaces

2 spaces

2 spaces

2 spaces

2 spaces

4 spaces

Figure 6.   Sample personal letter #1

```
                              Date


              Addressee's Name
              Street Address
              City, State Zip
2 spaces
              Salutation:
2 spaces
                   For a personal letter, you may want to use the less formal
              modified block style.
2 spaces
                   ..........................................................
                   ..........................................................
                   ..........................................................
2 spaces
                   Body single-spaced--2 spaces between paragraphs...........
                   ..........................................................
                   ..........................................................

                                   Best regards,                 2 spaces

                                                                  4 spaces

                                   Your name
                                   Street address
                                   City, State Zip
                                   Telephone (if desired)
```

Figure 7.   Sample personal letter #2

RESUMES

In arranging the information to be included in your resume, refer to the sample forms in Figures 8 and 9, experimenting with the format until it comes out right.

When typing a resume, it is important to consolidate the information on one page if possible. Prospective employers prefer one-page resumes.

If an attempt to do this produces unsightly overcrowding, for the sake of appearance, you must carry over to more pages.

SCHOOL PAPERS

Most college professors now require that students type all term papers, theses, and other written material. But typing school papers does not have to wait until college. Elementary and high school students should also submit typed papers whenever possible. Learning how to type and using your new skill for school is one step closer to neater

RÉSUMÉ

Name
Address
City, State Zip   Telephone:

CAREER
OBJECTIVE: To obtain an entry-level management position in
               personnel staffing.

EDUCATION:

Fall 1980   Jersey City State College, Jersey City, New Jersey
               Master of Arts Candidate

June 1975   Kean College, Union, New Jersey
               Bachelor of Arts, Education
               Cum Laude

               American Institute of Banking
               Newark, New Jersey

SKILLS: ADMINISTRATION AND MANAGEMENT
                 Supervise staff, budgets and facilities in non-profit
                 organization.

                 Attend to detail; challenged by making systems work;
                 gather sophisticated information and compile into
                 precise records as research assistant.

EXPERIENCE:

July 1979 -   Jersey City State College, Jersey City, New Jersey
Present   Responsibilities:
                 Right to Read Adult Reading Academy - Established
                 through interview, testing, diagnosis, and evaluation,
                 individualized programs to assist underprepared adults
                 in Reading and Math.
                 Candidates for GED.

                 Reading Improvement Center - Instruction given to college
                 freshmen in Reading and Study Skills Course. Personalized
                 instructive methods to meet specific needs of each student.

August 1976 - Roosevelt Junior High School, Westfield, New Jersey
July 1979   Compensatory Education Math Teacher

Sept. 1974 -   Roselle Board of Education, Roselle, New Jersey
July 1976   Reading Clinic - As a clinician, tested, diagnosed,
                 evaluated students for inter-disciplinary child-study
                 team which considered the contribution of socio-
                 environmental, intellectual, emotional, physical, and
                 educational factors particular to the client's problems.

PROFESSIONAL
AFFILIATIONS: New Jersey Educational Association.

REFERENCES: Available on request.

Figure 8. Sample résumé #1

RÉSUMÉ

NAME
Address
City, State Zip   Telephone

Experience

JERSEY CITY STATE COLLEGE, Jersey City, New Jersey (July 1979 to Present)

     Right to Read Adult Reading Academy--Established through interview,
testing, diagnosis, and evaluation, individualized programs to assist
underprepared adults in Reading and Math. Candidates for GED.

     Reading Improvement Center--Instruction given to college freshmen in
Reading and Study Skills Course. Personalized instructive methods to
meet specific needs of each student.

ROOSEVELT JUNIOR HIGH SCHOOL, Westfield, New Jersey (August 1976 to July 1979)

     Compensatory Education Math Teacher

ROSELLE BOARD OF EDUCATION, Roselle, New Jersey (Sept. 1974 to July 1976)

     Reading Clinic--As a clinician, tested, diagnosed, evaluated students
for inter-disciplinary child-study team which considered the contribution
of socio-environmental, intellectual, emotional, physical, and educational
factors particular to the client's problems.

Education

JERSEY CITY STATE COLLEGE, Jersey City, New Jersey (Fall 1980)

     Master of Arts Candidate

KEAN COLLEGE, Union, New Jersey (June 1975)

     Bachelor of Arts, Education
     Cum Laude

AMERICAN INSTITUTE OF BANKING, Newark, New Jersey

Skills

ADMINISTRATION AND MANAGEMENT

     Supervise staff, budgets and facilities in non-profit organization.

     Attend to detail; challenged by making systems work; gather sophisticated
     information and compile into precise records as research assistant.

References (Available on request)

Figure 9.   Sample résumé #2

papers and better grades.

The following illustrations and instructions may be used for papers in elementary and high school as well as college. The formats shown demonstrate all the main parts of any term paper, report, or thesis.

Title pages

Almost every report, term paper, or thesis requires a title page. Its function is to identify the name of the paper, the author and also the course and instructor. In a thesis or dissertation, this page also serves to state the educational degree to be achieved by the writer with presentation of the work.

There are other variations in format--some simpler, some more difficult. Check your class or school handbook for the exact format you need.

For a practice exercise, insert a page into your typewriter and copy the sample title pages shown in Figures 10, 11 and 12, using the exact spacing indicated. In doing this exercise, it would

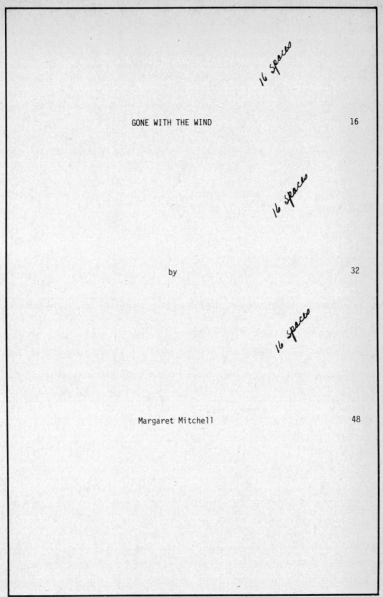

GONE WITH THE WIND   16

16 spaces

16 spaces

by   32

16 spaces

Margaret Mitchell   48

Figure 10.   Sample title page #1

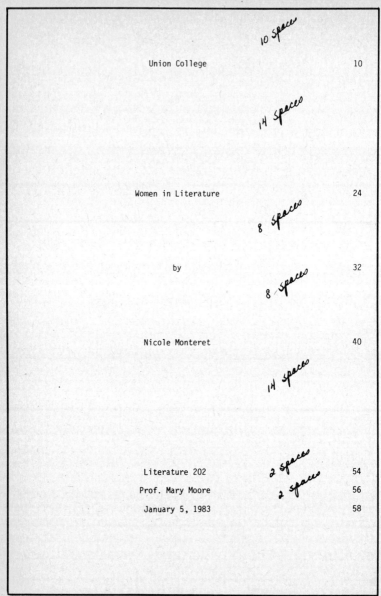

Union College   10

                              14 Spaces

Women in Literature   24

                              8 Spaces

by   32

                              8 Spaces

Nicole Monteret   40

                              14 Spaces

Literature 202   2 Spaces   54
Prof. Mary Moore   2 Spaces   56
January 5, 1983   58

Figure 11. Sample title page #2

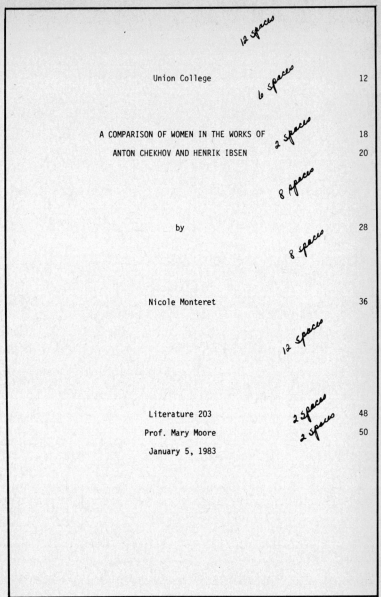

Union College   12

                                                 12 spaces
                                                 6 spaces

A COMPARISON OF WOMEN IN THE WORKS OF   18
ANTON CHEKHOV AND HENRIK IBSEN   20
                                                 2 spaces
                                                 8 spaces

                    by   28
                                                 8 spaces

             Nicole Monteret   36
                                                 12 spaces

             Literature 203   48
             Prof. Mary Moore   50
             January 5, 1983   _2 spaces_
                                                 2 spaces

Figure 12. Sample title page #3

BASIC FORMS   183

be wise to use the Vertical Guide Strip
even though the lines are indicated on
the samples. It will give you the feel
of using this aid in your work.

    After copying the sample title pages,
try your hand at these:

        New York University
        New Methods in Teaching Languages
        by
        Susan E. Williams
        Communications 6421
        Professor Eleanor Smith
        May 10, 1984

        Abraham Clark High School
        The History of American Labor Unionism
        by
        Jacqueline Holt
        History 10th Grade
        Prof. Elliot Eberhard
        May 10, 1984

Titled and untitled text pages

Figure 13 illustrates the basic format for the first page of most papers you will write. This format changes slightly if the work is divided into chapters. (See Figure 17 for an example of a chapter title page.)

Figure 14 illustrates the change in text setup which is to be used for all untitled pages in the test and reference sections.

Typing instructions

1) Begin all first pages or chapter or section headings twelve spaces down from the top of the page.

2) Type page numbers at the bottom of <u>all titled pages</u> including chapter beginnings, bibliographies, etc. On <u>all untitled pages</u>, type the page number at the top either centered or at the upper right hand corner, according to the form book you are following.

3) Set the left margin 12-15 spaces from the left edge and the right margin

Chapter 1

12 spaces

3 spaces

THE PROBLEM AND DEFINITIONS OF TERMS USED

3 spaces

Labor problems and grievances are as old as the
employment relationship itself. Humanity is such that,
always, there must have existed some discontentedness over
working conditions. More often than not, the worker was
not free to disclose his occupational grudge. To do so would
have cost him his employment. Freedom of expression came
with the establishment of formal grievance procedures. These
stretch back to 1892 when the Local Typographical Union and
the Chicago Publishers Association agreed, "...that all disputes arising out of the interpretation of the contract
should be settled by conciliation and arbitration." In 1901,
the International Publishers Association negotiated a nation-
wide plan for the settlement of disputes. This was followed
in 1902 by a like agreement between the same association and
the International Printers' Union.

In 1903 the coal and glass industries, and in 1911
the clothing industry established grievance procedures. The
success of the venture in these industries encouraged further
industrial acceptance of grievances machinery. Growth was
slow, however, and as late as 1919, the steel industry had
not yet established a system for settling grievances. There
gradually developed the general realization that if efficient

6 spaces

Figure 13. Sample first page for term paper
thesis
dissertation

6 spaces

- 2 -

3 spaces

The first signs of civilization in Ireland date back
to 6000 B.C. These stone age people gave the island its
ancient court monuments and portal dolmens. Next came the
Celts who gave Ireland the basis for its clans, language
and mysticism. Then came the Danes who, integrating with
the Celts, gave Ireland's children their red hair. Then,
the giving stopped and the taking began.

In 800 A.D. the Vikings began hit and run raids,
eventually establishing colonies for inland raids. They
were finally driven from the country in 1014.

Then, Hadrian IV, the only English pope, gave Ireland
to Henry II. The Normans, with Henry's permission, invaded,
driving the Danes out and eventually settling there. Through
generations, intermarriages with the Irish and mutual hatred
for the English, the Normans became totally Irish and joined
forces with the Celts against England. Henry VIII's retalia-
tion was swift and total. But, more important, his break
with Rome pinned identifying badges of Catholicism and
Protestantism on two growing, opposing factions.

At the end of the 16th century, Ulster Chieftains
tried unsuccessfully to rid Ireland of the English. These
defeated Chieftains fled to Europe and England immediately
claimed their land--bringing in a flood of English and
Scottish Protestant settlers.

1602 marked the end of the Norman and Celtic Ireland.
An eleven-year rebellion in 1641 reduced the population by

6 spaces

Figure 14. Sample untitled page

at 8-10 spaces from the right edge.   Indent paragraphs 5 or 6 spaces.

One simple matter of form. When beginning a new paragraph near the bottom
of a page, be sure you can fit at least
two lines of the new paragraph at the
bottom of the page in your typewriter
and that at least two lines will carry
over to the top of the next page.   If
this is not possible, do not begin the
paragraph on the page in your typewriter,
even if it means leaving the page a bit
shorter in text than the rest.   In this
case, a short page is not only permissi-
ble, but is preferred over poor form.

Poor form

     In 1903 the coal and glass industries,

          (end of page)

Correct form

     In 1903 the coal and glass industries,
and in 1911 the clothing industry, set up
          (end of page)

End Notes or References

This type of listing is used when a paper has reference numbers indicated in the text but the references are not entered at the bottom of the page as footnotes. Instead, all reference sources are entered in a body of one or more pages at the end of the paper.

Because of its simplicity, this easy form is usually used with short college papers and with most reports or term papers for grades below college level.

Typing instructions

Indent 6 spaces for the first line of each item. Type the reference number $\frac{1}{2}$ space above the line. Begin typing the first word leaving no space between number and word. Type all items in single space unless otherwise indicated by your instructor or form book. If note runs more than one typed line, all lines after the first begin at the margin. Double space between items. This is how your first item should look:

END NOTES

[1]H.M. Alden (Memorandum on "Project of Novel by Henry James") cited in S.P. Rosenbaum, ed., <u>Henry James The Ambassadors</u> (New York: W.W. Norton and Company, 1964), p. 413.

[2]Lewis Leary, Introduction to <u>The Awakening</u> by Kate Chopin (New York: Holt, Rinehart and Winston, Inc., 1970), xvii.

[3]Edmund Wilson, <u>Patriotic Gore</u> (New York: Oxford University Press, 1962), p. 591.

[4]Henry James, <u>The Ambassadors</u> (New York: New American Library, 1960), p. 13.

[5]Kate Chopin, <u>The Awakening</u> (New York; W.W. Norton and Company, 1976), p. 14.

[6]Per Seyerstead, <u>The Complete Works of Kate Chopin</u> (Baton Rouge: Louisiana State Press, 1969), p. 24.

[7]Per Seyerstead, <u>Kate Chopin: A Critical Biography</u> (Baton Rouge: Louisiana State University Press, 1969), p. 143.

[8]F.O. Matthiessen, "The Ambassadors," <u>S.P. Rosenbaum, Henry James the Ambassadors</u>, (New York: W.W. Norton and Company, 1964), p. 15.

[9]F.O. Matthiessen, p. 429.

14

Figure 15. Sample end note page

BASIC FORMS

H.M. Alden (Memorandum on "Project on Novel by Henry James") cited in S.P. Rosenbaum, ed., The Ambassadors by Henry James (New York: W.W. Norton and Company, 1964), p. 413.

If the references fill more than one page, type the titled page using the space and placement illustrated in Figure 15. On all subsequent pages, place the page number at the top in the center or at the upper right hand corner, as typed in the previous pages of text, and begin the first line of type down the usual number of spaces for all untitled pages.

Bibliographies

This section lists all or most of the research materials used in writing a paper. In some cases, only the important sources will be listed. This would then be called a "Selected Bibliography" or some other title indicating that not all materials used in research have been listed.

Many kinds of research sources may be

BIBLIOGRAPHY

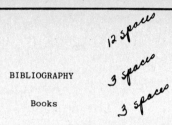

Books

Everson, William K. The Art of W.C. Fields. New York:
Bonanza Books, 1967.

Yanni, Nicholas. W.C. Fields. New York: Pyramid Communications, Inc. 1974.

Articles

Broun, Heywood. "W.C. Fields and the Cosmos." Nation 132
(January 7, 1931), p. 24.

Cerf, Bennett. "Trade Winds." Saturday Review 27 (June 3
1944), p. 20.

Ferguson, Otis. "Great McGonigle." New Republic 84 (August 21,
1935), p. 48.

_____. "Comedian in New Screen Role after Winning Back
His Health." Literary Digest 121 (June 20, 1936)
p. 19.

_____. "The Old Fashioned Way." New Republic 103
(December 30, 1940), p. 900.

_____. "Happy Landings." New Republic 105 (November 10,
1941), p. 622.

Ford, C. "One and Only W.C. Fields." Harper 235 (October,
1967), p. 65.

Flatley, Guy. "Who Was He?" New York Times Magazine.
(April 24, 1966), p. 114.

Handlin, O. "Fear and Laughter." Atlantic 221 (January,
1968), p. 116.

Markfield, Wallace. "Dark Geography of W.C. Fields."
New York Times Magazine (April 24, 1966), pp. 32,
110-120.

57

Figure 16. Sample bibliography page

used--books, periodicals, interviews, etc. In typing, note the spacing and captioning of each group as illustrated in Figure 16.

Typing instructions

The first line of each source begins at the margin. Every line of type after the first is indented 6 spaces. All items are typed in single space, but double space between items.

If two or more works by the same author are used, do not repeat author's name when entering the sources after the first one. Correct form requires that you type a line 8 spaces long ended by a period. The line should begin at the margin. Type the title of the next work as usual. Your entries should look like this:

Ferguson, Otis. "Great McGonigal." New
     Republic 84 (August 21, 1935), p.48.

_____. "Comedian in New Screen Role
     after Winning Back His Health."
     Literary Digest 121 (June 20, 1936),
     p. 19.

Occasionally, you may be required to do an "Annotated Bibliography." This lists sources and also comments on each work in some way. Type as instructed above, indenting an extra 2 spaces for the first line of the comment. This type of entry should look like this:

Markfield, Wallace. "Dark Geography of W.C. Fields," New York Times Maga-zine (April 24, 1966), pp. 32, 110-120.
    An admirable work which illus-trates the genius of the man as a comedian and observer of life.

Note: A bibliography must be typed in alphabetical order.

Footnotes

Now that you've discovered you can do the straight typing, you have the con-fidence you need for the tricky part of college papers--fitting footnotes at the bottom of a page and knowing exactly how much space to leave. (See Figures 17 and 18 for examples of the finished pro-ducts.) This is the one requirement that stops most people cold and makes them afraid to type their own footnoted papers. It seems so complicated.

This is no longer true. The following simple, easy-to-use, foolproof method works on every page. To learn it, follow the instructions step by step.

Typing instructions

1) Taking your Vertical Guide Strip (see pages 131 and 132) and a sheet of paper, insert both into your typewriter side by side with the guide either to the left or right of the page. Make sure that the top edges are lined up.

2) Begin to type your text. When you reach the first footnote, enter this footnote number in the standard way-- like this.[1]

3) Check the reference sheet for footnote #1. Estimate the number of

---

[1]How to Start a Profitable Typing Service--at Home, by Nicki Montaperto (New York: Barnes & Noble Books, 1981), p. 83.

typed lines you will need, remembering
that footnotes are typed single spaced.
Judging by eye, for the page size of this
book, footnote #1 required 4 typed lines,
as set up on the preceding page where it
first appeared referenced in the text.
(When you're working with a standard
$8\frac{1}{2}$ x 11-inch sheet, the same footnote
would probably require 2 typed lines.)
Write this number down. Add the 8 spaces
you need for the bottom margin and the 2
spaces for the dividing line. Totaling
the three figures tells you how many
lines you need to fit this footnote
properly. With a glance at your numbered
Vertical Guide Strip, you can tell how
many spaces you have left on the page.
If you are only on line 27 or anywhere
above the line where you must start
typing the footnote, continue typing.

    4) If you reach another footnote,
stop! Before you type the line containing this new footnote number, be sure
there is room for the reference at the
bottom of the page. This is a form

requirement.[2] Every footnote indicated in the text <u>must be</u> referenced at the bottom of the page on which it is noted. If there is not enough room to fit the reference for the new footnote coming up in the next line of text, end on the line above, even if it means that this page will be a little shorter than some of the others.   The method to figure out space for more than one reference at the bottom of the page and an illustration of the way it should look appears on page 199.

5) When using footnotes, if the last page is short in text, figure out the space you need for any footnotes appearing in the text on the last page and drop to that place at the end of the page to type the footnotes, disregarding the width of the space left between the end of the text.and the footnotes.

---

[2]<u>A Manual for Writers of Term Papers, Theses and Dissertations,</u> Fourth Edition, by Kate L. Turabian (Chicago: The University of Chicago Press, 1973), p. 79.

This is how the last page would look if there wasn't room for the next footnote or if this was the last page of the paper. Footnote #2 noted on page 197 is repeated here for illustration.

---

[2]A Manual for Writers of Term Papers, Theses and Dissertations, Fourth Edition, by Kate L. Turabian (Chicago: The University of Chicago Press, 1973), p. 79.

BASIC FORMS

6) To figure out space for more than one footnote at the bottom of the page, use this method:

Dividing line	2	spaces
Bottom margin	8	"
Footnote #1	4	"
Space between footnotes	2	"
Footnote #2	4	"
	20	"

To include the two references that were cited on pages 195 and 197 at the bottom of a page this size (containing a total of 48 single spaced lines) would require 20 lines of space. For practice purposes, pretend they were on the same page. Keep typing to line 22 on the Vertical Guide Strip. On line 20, type

----

[1]How to Start a Profitable Typing Service--at Home, by Nicki Montaperto (New York: Barnes & Noble Books, 1981), p. 83.

[2]A Manual for Writers of Term Papers, Theses and Dissertations, Fourth Edition, by Kate L. Turabian (Chicago: The University of Chicago Press, 1973), p. 79.

a solid line 2½ inches long (about twenty spaces), a form requirement for separating the text from the footnotes.

On line 18, type the number "1" about ½ space above the line. With no space interval, begin typing the first reference. (Remember footnotes are typed single spaced unless otherwise required by your instructor or form manual. If they are to be typed double spaced, make allowances in adding the number of spaces you need for each footnote.)

After you complete the first reference, leave a double space between footnote #1 and #2, a form requirement. Type the number "2" about ½ space above the line and continue typing as with footnote #1.

And that's all there is to it. If it sounds complicated, actually doing it will clear up any confusion.

With two or more footnotes at the bottom, your 8½ x 11-inch page (containing a total of 66 lines of space from top to bottom) should look like Figures 17 and 18 on pages 201 and 202.

Chapter 1

10 spaces

INTRODUCTION

3 spaces

3 spaces

On December 23, 1971 the Federal Communications
Commission announced it was dismissing proceedings in
which it would have investigated several crucial aspects
of the rates of the American Telephone and Telegraph
Company and the Associated Bell System Companies for inter-
state service. The matters that were to have been examined
included revenue requirements, reasonableness of Western
Electric's (AT&T's wholly owned subsidiary) prices and pro-
fits, and the amounts claimed by the carrier for investment
and operating expenses.[1] The original impetus for examining
these matters went back at least to 1965, when the FCC had
begun its first formal investigation of AT&T's rate struc-
ture.[2]

The decision to dismiss the investigation was widely
regarded as an admission of regulatory failure. Senator
Fred R. Harris said the FCC had "surrendered to bigness."[3]

_____

2 spaces
2 spaces

[1]American Telephone and Telegraph Company, Charges
for Domestic Service (Docket No. 19129, F.C.C. 71-1284),
32 F.C.C. 2d 691 (1971).

2 spaces

[2]Letter from Dean Burch, F.C.C. Chairman, January 13,
1972, 118 Cong. Rec. 70 (1972).

2 spaces

[3]Letter from Senator Fred R. Harris to Dean Burch,
January 1, 1972, 118 Cong. Rec. 69 (1972).

3 spaces
1
5 spaces

Figure 17. Sample first page with footnotes

1966 an inquiry into the establishment of domestic communications satellites by non-common carriers.[105] Obligingly,
the FCC did not complete its own inquiry until the Johnson
Task Force had made its report in December 1968. In early
1969 the FCC was prepared to authorize a Comsat managed
pilot domestic communications satellite program as recommended
in the Task Force Report. A draft of the FCC report and
order was taken to the White House staff by then Chairman
Hyde. By that time, it was the Nixon White House rather
than the Johnson White House. The FCC was asked to hold
back on any action until the policy questions were reexamined
by the new men in the White House. The reexamination resulted
in the January 23, 1970 memorandum from Peter Flanigan which
we discussed above.[106]

On March 20, 1970 the FCC approved a report[107] which
concluded that it had the power to authorize any non-Fede-
ral Government entity, whether a common carrier or not, to

---

[105]Establishment of Domestic Non-common Carrier
Communications--Satellite Facilities by Nongovernmental
Entities (Docket No. 16495), 2 F.C.C. 2d 668.

[106]For the Peter Flanigan memorandum and a very help-
ful article by Bruce E. Thorp see notes 99 and 98 respectively.
Further information is to be found in the Concurring Opinion
of Commissioner Nicholas Johnson to Establishment of Domestic
Communication--Satellite Facilities by Nongovernmental Entities (Docket No. 16495), 35 F.C.C. 2d 863 (1972).

[107]Establishment of Domestic Communication--Satellite
Facilities by Nongovernmental Entities (Docket No. 16495)
22 F.C.C. 2d 86 (1970).

Figure 18. Sample second page with footnotes

MANUSCRIPTS

For writers, learning how to type is
absolutely essential, and not just for
the final copy to be submitted to an
editor for consideration or publication.
Every word from the first page of the
first draft should be done on the typewriter whenever possible. Learning to
work this way will enable a writer to
produce more work. The copy will also
be easier to work with for editing than
handwritten drafts could ever be. Learning to write directly on a typewriter
takes a little practice, but in the end,
it's worth learning. There are some
little tricks to enable you to master
this important technique. The method
can, and should, be used by students too
in writing school papers of all kinds.

Composing on a typewriter for writers and students

Once you become fully accustomed to
typing, you may find that you become im-
patient when you are trying to write a
long composition or other material which

must be typed in the final form. Doing the first draft and all other drafts on the typewriter will save you a lot of time. At first, it may seem awkward to type your thoughts. Two easy steps will soon enable you to put your thoughts into type even more easily than you did in pen or pencil because it will be so much faster.

1) Set your typewriter on triple spacing. If your typewriter does not have a triple space but has 1½ space adjustment, set it on 1½ and space twice between lines to give yourself the needed three spaces. On typewriters with only single and double spacing, set the typewriter on double spacing and hit the carriage return twice at the end of a line to give you four spaces between lines.

2) Roll a piece of paper into the typewriter and start writing the material just as it flows from you. Do not stop to edit or change anything. Keep going to the end. Don't stop this creative flow for anything. If you have already

written a sentence or a paragraph, or
even a scene, in one way and a better
way of saying it occurs to you, don't
stop to take out the first way you've
typed it. Simply type in the second
form and keep on going to the end.

3) After the entire piece of writing
is done in the first draft, go back to
the beginning and start editing, changing,
or reorganizing it with pen or pencil.
By triple spacing, you have left yourself
plenty of room between lines for changes.
A list of editing symbols and practice
exercise are on pages 163 and 164.

4) In reorganizing your first draft,
retype pages only when they become il-
legible from heavy editing. Use the cut
and paste method for moving parts around,
cutting a section out from its original
position and pasting or stapling it into
the spot where you wish to move it.

Once you learn to work this way, you
will find first drafts of anything will
become easier and be completed more
quickly than when working with pen and
pencil.

Setting up a manuscript

Typing instructions

The following format may be used for any article, story, or book manuscript to be submitted to a publisher:

1) Use white 20-lb. bond paper either with or without rag content, depending on how much money you want to spend.

2) Plan to make a carbon copy or to photocopy the original. (Never send your only copy out to a publisher.)

3) Set your typewriter on double space and leave it there.

4) Set your left margin 1½ inches from the left edge and the right margin 1 inch from the right edge. Leave no less than 1 inch of space at the top and bottom of the page.

5) In the upper left hand corner of the first page of text, type your name and address. In the upper right hand corner, type the number of words in the manuscript. (Calculate this by counting the words on three pages to get an average word per page count and multiply

Author's Name   Approximate Word Count
Address
City, State Zip
Telephone (if desired)

24 spaces

                    TITLE OF MANUSCRIPT
            2 spaces   by
            2 spaces
                            Pen Name   (if different from above)
            3 spaces
        In today's world, typing is probably the next most

needed service after sex and cooking.   Today's world revolves

on paper work.   That means freelance typists are more in de-

mand than ever before and the need is growing all the time.

        Who should consider starting this business?   Anybody

who knows how to type, needs extra money for any reason,

wants to work at home at flexible hours and needs to start a

business requiring a small capital outlay to begin.

        Who can go into this simple business?   Anybody who

knows how to type.   You don't need great speed.   Your speed

will develop as you go along.   You're working at home.

                        - more -

                5 spaces

Figure 19.   Sample first page - manuscript

5 spaces 2 3 spaces

Nobody is watching how fast you produce. You have only to
turn out good, neat copy which will keep people coming back
for more and/or recommending you to others.

You don't need a terrific typewriter. Be it the
most humble manual or the most sophisticated electronic
word processor, all you need is a typewriter that will produce clean, neat copy.

You don't need an elaborate work area. A kitchen
table is as good a place to start as any and you can build
toward bigger and better setups as your income and workload
increase.

What you do need is confidence in yourself to get
started.

If it sounds complicated, it isn't. Just take one
job at a time, learn what you need to accomplish that one
job. If you make a mistake--so what? Just retype the page,
or the whole job if need be, and go on to the next a little
more expert than you were before you started.

The main thing to remember is that your business will
be slow in starting but will build up gradually as your repu-
tation spreads. And spread it will if you produce quality work.

If you are conscientious and persevering, you'll soon
be winging along, page after page, in a job where you are
your own boss, working whatever hours you decide, for however
many hours you decide, in a money-making venture that cost
you almost nothing to get started.

- more -

5 spaces

Figure 20.   Sample subsequent page - manuscript

Chapter 4

When Julie woke the next morning, it was pouring
outside. She stood at her favorite window and looked out
but the mist was too thick to see even as far as the lake--
a perfect day to bury herself in writing. But her appoint-
ment with Alec was uppermost in her mind. She smiled to
herself as she questioned the cause of her eagerness. Was
she really that anxious to go over the accounts and other
business details regarding The Parsonage?

"It's both," she decided, lying playfully to herself
and went cheerfully down to breakfast.

"Good morning," Cedric said as she arrived in the
dining room. "You're a welcome bright sight on a dull,
rainy morning."

Julie smiled. It was exactly why she had chosen the
bright yellow print blouse and yellow slacks. She knew how

- more - 3 spaces
5 spaces

Figure 21.   Sample chapter page - manuscript

by the number of pages.)

6) Drop about 24 lines and center the title using horizontal centering. Type the title in solid capitals.

If you are not using a pen name, do not retype your name under the title. If your pen name is different from the name you typed at the top, go down 2 spaces from the title and type the word "by" in small letters in the center. Go down 2 more spaces and center your pen name using upper and lower case. (See Figure 19.)

7) Leave 3 spaces after the title or your pen name and begin typing the text, indenting 6 spaces for paragraphs.

8) When you are 1 inch from the bottom of the page, center the word "more" with a hyphen on each side to indicate to the typesetter that more material follows.

(- more -)

9) When starting the second and all subsequent pages, including chapter beginnings, type your last name in the upper left-hand corner and the page

number in the upper right-hand corner. This helps identify the work and its place in the manuscript if parts are misplaced or separated in the publisher's office or elsewhere.

10) Come down 3 single spaces from your last name and continue typing the text. (See Figure 20.)

11) If you are typing a book manuscript, the first page of each chapter is set up as the title page: i.e., the chapter number and chapter title, if any, are placed about 24 single spaces down from the top. Leave 3 more single spaces between the chapter title and the first line of text. (See Figure 21.)

12) When you reach the end of the manuscript, leave one or two double spaces from the last line of text and type the number "30" in the center. This is the standard symbol used to indicate to the typesetter that nothing more follows.

How to mail a manuscript to a publisher

1) Type the manuscript according to

the typing instructions for manuscripts.

2) If you have not made a carbon copy while typing the manuscript, have it photocopied and keep the copy for your files.

3) Make a record sheet of submissions, including the publisher's name, address, date sent, postage, and expected date of response for that publisher. (If a manuscript is out 5 or 6 weeks and you have heard nothing from the publisher, write a little note asking about its status.

4) Write a cover letter only if there is something special you need to say. Don't write a letter saying just that you are submitting the manuscript for the publisher's consideration and you hope they like it.

5) Prepare the manuscript for mailing according to the number of pages, and be sure to include a self-addressed stamped envelope to ensure that it is returned to you if the publisher cannot use it.

Use the following chart as a guide in preparing manuscripts of different lengths for mailing.

No. of Pages	Inside Envelope	Outside Envelope
1-4 (folded in thirds)	3-7/8" x 8-7/8" (No. 9)	4-1/8" x 9-1/2" (No. 10)
5-10 (folded in half)	6" x 9"	6½" x 9½"
10-200 (mailed flat)	9" x 12"	10" x 13"
200+ (mailed flat in a box with return postage enclosed)		

STENCILS

Stencils are used to reproduce material run off on a mimeograph machine.

Typing stencils

1) Before typing on the stencil itself, make a model of the work to be done using the same size paper and setup.

2) To type the stencil, move the ribbon selector to the stencil position. This disengages the ribbon and permits the keys or typing ball to strike the stencil directly, thus "cutting" the letter into the stencil. This cut permits the mimeograph ink to come through

in the mimeograph printing process.

3) Insert the cushion sheet with the glossy side up between the stencil sheet and the waxed backing sheet.

4) Roll the stencil into your typewriter just as you would a sheet of paper. Begin to type the stencil exactly as you set it up on your model.

Making corrections on stencils

1) Turn your roller up a few spaces above the error.

2) Brush a light coat of special correction fluid over the error and let it dry thoroughly. This fluid recoats the stencil, filling in the spaces cut in error.

3) When the fluid is dry, type the correct letter.

4) Proofread the stencil before removing it from the typewriter.

Drawing on stencils

Illustrations or handprinting on a stencil must be done with a special stylus, using a stylus with a head

designed for your specific need. You
will also need a special plastic backing
sheet. Both the stylus with a variety
of heads and the plastic backing sheet
may be purchased in any stationery store.

ADDRESSING ENVELOPES AND POST CARDS

Envelopes and post cards are available
in a variety of sizes. The most commonly
used sizes are:

- Small or letter size (6½ x 3-5/8
inches)
- Large or legal size (9½ x 4-1/8
inches)
- Post cards (5½ x 3¼ inches)

Standard Size Envelopes and Post Cards

Typing instructions (See Figures 22,
23, and 24.)

1) Return address. Move down 3
spaces from the top of the envelope or
card and 3 spaces from the left edge.
Type the return address single spaced in
block form.

2) Mailing address. Move down to 2
spaces above the vertical center of the

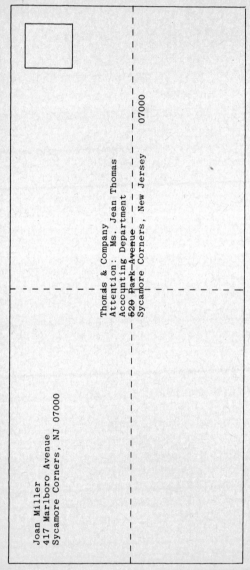

Figure 22. Sample legal envelope

BASIC FORMS

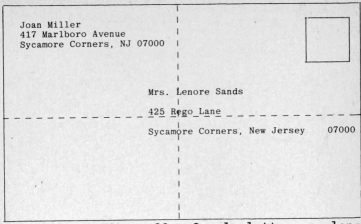

Figure 23.   Sample letter envelope

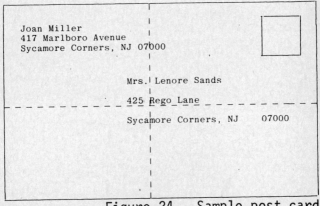

Figure 24.   Sample post card

envelope and 5 spaces to the left of the
horizontal center.

   3) Using block form, double space a
3-line address and single space for 4 or
more line addresses.

   4) Type the company name on the first
line.

   5) Type Attention, Personal, or any
similar notations on the second line followed by the person's name.

   6) Type department names, street address, and post office box numbers on the
following lines.

   7) Type the city, state, and zip code
leaving $\frac{1}{2}$-inch space between the state
and the zip code.

Addressing large envelopes

   When addressing envelopes too large
for the typewriter, type the address on a
label and paste in the center of the envelope.

   If the envelope does not have a
printed return address, type the return
address on another label and paste it in
the upper left hand corner.

Chainfeeding envelopes and post cards

When addressing a large number of envelopes or post cards, many typists use a method called chainfeeding to speed up the job.

1) Set the margins and tab stops needed for all the cards and envelopes to be addressed.

2) Stack the cards or envelopes on the side of the typewriter comfortable to you for inserting and removing.

3) Insert the first card or envelope into your typewriter and roll it into the machine. Stop just before the bottom edge disappears.

4) Insert another card or envelope between the roller and the edge sticking out. Continue to turn the roller until the first piece is in position.

5) Type the address, spacing up to each line as usual. As the first piece is moved up, the second piece will be drawn into the typewriter automatically.

6) When the first piece is typed, roll it out of the typewriter and insert a third card or envelope before the

bottom edge of the second piece disappears under the roller.

7) Continue typing, repeating all steps, until the stack of cards or envelopes is typed.

FOLDING LETTERS

Using letter-size envelopes (6½ x 3-5/8 inches)

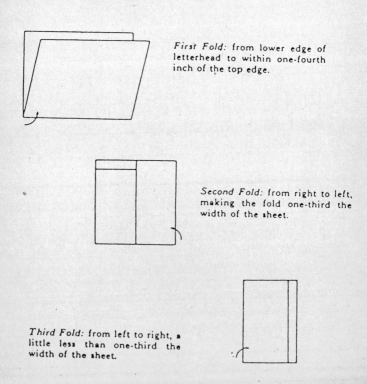

First Fold: from lower edge of letterhead to within one-fourth inch of the top edge.

Second Fold: from right to left, making the fold one-third the width of the sheet.

Third Fold: from left to right, a little less than one-third the width of the sheet.

BASIC FORMS

Using legal-size envelopes (9½ x 4-1/8 inches)

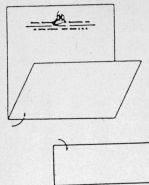

First Fold: from lower edge of letterhead to within a little less than one-third the distance from the top.

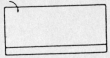

Second Fold: down to about one-fourth inch from the crease of the first fold.

Folding a letter for a window envelope

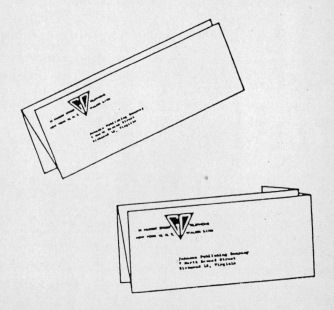

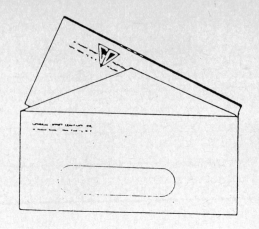

BASIC FORMS

NEW STATE ABBREVIATIONS

Alabama	AL	Montana	MT
Alaska	AK	Nebraska	NB
Arizona	AZ	Nevada	NV
Arkansas	AR	New Hampshire	NH
California	CA	New Jersey	NJ
Colorado	CO	New Mexico	NM
Connecticut	CT	New York	NY
Delaware	DE	North Carolina	NC
D.C.	DC	North Dakota	ND
Florida	FL	Ohio	OH
Georgia	GA	Oklahoma	OK
Hawaii	HI	Oregon	OR
Idaho	ID	Pennsylvania	PA
Illinois	IL	Puerto Rico	PR
Indiana	IN	Rhode Island	RI
Iowa	IA	South Carolina	SC
Kansas	KS	South Dakota	SD
Kentucky	KY	Tennessee	TN
Louisiana	LA	Texas	TX
Maine	ME	Utah	UT
Maryland	MD	Vermont	VT
Massachusetts	MA	Virginia	VA
Michigan	MI	Washington	WA
Minnesota	MN	West Virginia	WV
Mississippi	MS	Wisconsin	WI
Missouri	MO	Wyoming	WY

Type in solid capitals with no period at the end.

6

Typing Aids

MATERIALS AND SUPPLIES

As you begin to use your typewriter
more and more, you will want to know
more about supplies you will need for
different kinds of work. The following
list will give you some basic information about paper, ribbons, correcting
materials and other stationery supplies.
For more details, ask your local stationery or typewriter dealer.

Paper

In the last few years, paper prices
have skyrocketed. For this reason, you
should use expensive paper only when

necessary. For a simple term paper or similar material, you do not need top quality. White sulphite, a long grain white bond, is a good heavyweight paper which is easy to work with and presents a good appearance.

If you need to make a little better impression and don't mind the extra dollars, use a 20 lb. bond with 25 percent or more in rag content. This will cost much more but it is available in packs of 100 sheets if you need it just once in a while.

Paper is sold in reams of 500 sheets. If you plan to do a lot of typing, buying by the ream saves money. If you only need paper in small amounts, you can buy most any weight paper in packs of 100 sheets.

DON'T BUY ERASABLE BOND! Erasable paper is coated to prevent the ink of your ribbon from drying too fast. This makes errors flick off with a pencil eraser. But this non-absorbing feature also gives this paper a tendency to smudge and smear because the ink tends to rub off on everything that touches it--the bail rollers, your fingers, or anything else that may come into contact with your typed page. The correcting materials now available make the trouble and extra cost unnecessary. (See page 230.)

DO BUY ERASABLE ONION SKIN PAPER for carbon copies. Erasable onion skin is a thin, tissue-like coated paper. Here the extra money is well worth spending because easy erasing makes neater copies and saves lots of time, especially if you are making many carbon copies.

Carbon paper

Carbon paper is used between sheets to produce a copy of what you are typing. It comes in black or dark blue in a variety of qualities and inking techniques. It is also sold in different quantities in packs from 10 to 100 sheets.

The most convenient, though most expensive, is the new plastic film which makes up to 60 to 100 copies per sheet. This makes it less expensive in the long

run over lower priced types. In addition, this film is extremely clean to
work with and does not blacken your finger tips.

Money saving tip in stretching your carbon paper

After you have used a sheet of carbon
paper many times, if you examine it
closely, you will see heavily inked areas
still remain between the lines. To get
further use from the sheet, cut a $\frac{1}{4}$-inch
strip off the end. This will reposition
the carbon between the pages so that
this space between the lines will be
utilized. The copy will look like a new
carbon has been used. One problem--this
works only with double spacing because
single spaced copy uses all the lines on
the carbon paper.

Typewriter ribbons

Cotton. This is the least expensive,
will give you a dark impression and will
last a long time but you'll spend a lot

of time cleaning your keys. It sheds
lint which becomes trapped in your keys.

   Nylon and silk. Next in price, this
will give you a lighter impression than
cotton, but will last a long time and
give a clear, sharp impression without
the cleaning problems of a cotton ribbon.
This doesn't mean your keys won't ever
need cleaning. But the problem is defi-
nitely worse with cotton.

   Carbon ribbon. This is a one-time use
ribbon which is more expensive than fabric ribbon but has certain advantages. A
carbon ribbon produces copy that is the
same shade of print on every page. This
is important when typing a long work such
as a dissertation which must be published
for the university and gains in appearance
if every page is the same shading. It
is also important if a change must be
made in the middle of a long manuscript.
Retyped pages or corrections within a
page will never stand out because of a
difference in shading.

If you have a typewriter with a built-in correcting device and you want completely invisible corrections, this is the only type of ribbon you may use because the correcting lift-off tape works only with a carbon ribbon.

Tech III. This is one other ribbon you should know about if you are using a Selectric typewriter--one with a typing ball. It is not a carbon ribbon and can now be used with its own coverup correcting tape on your correcting mechanism as well. The advantage is that this multi-strike ribbon (meaning characters overlap on the ribbon space) goes through the typewriter at a slower pace, thus yielding almost triple the typing for far less than triple the price.

This less expensive ribbon is usually suitable for most kinds of work, especially for first drafts or practice setups.

Ask your typewriter supply service people to demonstrate and explain the different types of ribbons available for your machine. It may save you money and will assure you of using the ribbons best suited to your needs and your typewriter.

Correcting devices and materials

We all make mistakes. As the saying goes, that's why pencils have erasers. Try all the following correcting materials and stick with the ones that work the neatest and best for you.

Correcting fluids. These go on with a brush, dry almost instantly, and are now available in colors as well as white (for colored paper). For whiting out large areas, they're great. But if appearance is important, use them only if the bottle has been well capped and the liquid is thin and smooth. Once the bottle has been opened dozens of times or has been left uncapped, the fluid thickens, goes on lumpy, and typing over it will look sloppy. When this happens, buy a fresh bottle.

<u>Chalk backed correcting strips.</u> This
is chalked paper available in strips or
sheets. The strip is inserted with the
chalked side directly against the paper
over the error. The error is retyped to
cover it. The strip is then removed and
the correct letter typed over the whited
out error, leaving a clean, almost invisible correction. This is best for mistakes no longer than a word or two.

· The problem with this method is that
the chalk tends to flake off into your
typewriter. Clean your typewriter often
to prevent buildup.

This type of chalked tape is also now
available in spools to fit typewriters
with a built-in correcting feature and
is suitable for use with the Tech III
non-carbon ribbon.

<u>Self Adhesive Correcting Tape.</u> When
correcting an error involving one or
more full lines of type, cut a strip off
the roll the length of the line of type
and retype the new line or lines directly
onto the correction strip. This is

especially good for photocopying or photo offset masters.

Correcting lift-off tape. This is used strictly on machines with a built-in correction device. Corrections are literally invisible, whether you change one letter, a whole word, or an entire line. How does it do that?

The correcting tape has an adhesive backing. It works only with carbon ribbons. When the correcting feature on the typewriter is engaged, the adhesive backing literally picks the letter off the page, leaving the spot perfectly clean to receive the correct letter.

This feature increases the cost of your typewriter considerably but it's well worth the price for the quality of copy it produces.

Correcting ribbon cartridge. Some of the newer electric portables now operate with a ribbon cartridge which holds either a fabric ribbon which can be used until it wears out because it runs back and forth continuously or with a ribbon which goes through only once. To make corrections on this ribbon, you may purchase a separate cartridge which holds only correction tape. The problem here is that in order to make invisible corrections, you have to remove the ribbon cartridge, insert the correcting cartridge, cover the error, and then switch back to the ribbon cartridge to continue working.

Half-and-half ribbons. These are ribbons which are inked across the top half but have the correcting strip running across the bottom half. To make corrections, you simply change the ribbon position selector on your typewriter to allow you to type on the bottom half of the ribbon. This is available both in spools and cartridges which means that you can obtain this for almost any typewriter you're using and it's a lot more convenient than switching cartridges.

Find out what's available

The only way to know everything available for your typewriter is to check your typewriter or stationery supply store. Ask questions and experiment with everything and anything that comes out until you have found the method of making corrections that is best for you.

Copy stands to ease eye strain

One item which should be in your first purchase of supplies, especially if you plan to do a lot of typing, is a copy stand to hold your copy work upright instead of placing it flat on the desk or table next to your typewriter. This is a much easier and more correct angle for your eyes in reading the material--especially if you have many pages to do or are working with copy that is hard to follow. They cost no more than about $2.00 and are well worth it for diminished eyestrain.

If you prefer to make your own, here's how.

Cut two pieces of cardboard. Make
one 6 x 8 inches and the other 6 x 10
inches. Fold the two-inch strip up on
the longer piece. This will provide a
little shelf to stand the work on.

Tape the two pieces of cardboard together at the top. Cut two pieces of
string or yarn about 4 inches long. Tape
one end of the string to each board about
halfway down. Repeat on the other side
with the other string.

When opened out, it should stand something like a picture frame and the im-
provised copy stand will work perfectly.

Copy tip

Large paper clips will hold a book or
other unwieldy copy material firmly in
place on your copy stand.